P9-BIE-297

SOPHOCLES
THREE TRAGEDIES

No performance or reading of any of these plays may
be given unless a license has been obtained in advance
from the translator's American representative,
Miss Toby Cole, 234 West 44th Street,
New York 36, New York

SOPHOCLES
THREE TRAGEDIES

ANTIGONE • OEDIPUS THE KING • ELECTRA

TRANSLATED INTO ENGLISH VERSE BY

H. D. F. KITTO

OXFORD UNIVERSITY PRESS

LONDON • OXFORD • NEW YORK

OXFORD UNIVERSITY PRESS
Oxford   London   New York
Glasgow   Toronto   Melbourne   Wellington
Cape Town   Salisbury   Ibadan   Nairobi   Lusaka   Addis Ababa
Bombay   Calcutta   Madras   Karachi   Lahore   Dacca
Kuala Lumpur   Hong Kong   Tokyo

English translations, Preface and Selection © Oxford University Press, 1962
First published as an Oxford University Press paperback, 1962

This reprint, 1969

Printed in the United States of America

PREFACE

Of the three translations here offered, those of the *Antigone* and *Electra* were written, like their originals, for immediate stage-production. I hope they resemble the originals in some other respects too, though Sophocles' style is so supple, with such constant and dramatic variation of diction, rhythm, pace, and tension that no translator dare pitch his hopes very high. In translating, I accepted certain restrictions, as a matter of feeling rather than of theory – though in fact I think the modern doctrine that a new translation must be contemporary in style is fallacious in theory and dull in practice: Sophocles is not a contemporary of ours, and if he were he could not write these plays; and his style never was 'contemporary' but was his own. I have used a fairly strict metre, I have not allowed myself a greater number of verses than Sophocles used, and where he is formal – as in the line-by-line dialogue – I too have been formal. The translation of the *Antigone* was made for a production in which the lyric parts were to be sung; Sophocles' own lyric rhythms in this play are so dramatic that it seemed presumptuous to try to find better ones; therefore I followed them as closely as the English language permits. Elsewhere I have represented the original rhythmic structure of the lyrics only approximately, though observing fairly closely the correspondence of strophe with antistrophe. These restraints certainly made things more difficult, for which very reason the translations, whatever they may be worth, have more life than they would have had otherwise.

One reason for eschewing modern verse techniques was that the plays are so passionate, and passion, as the Greeks knew well, is the more powerfully expressed by being kept under strict formal control. Another reason was the matter of 'distancing'. These plays have size; they are not concerned simply with tragic individuals caught in a particular tragic situation, not simply with the character and fate of a Tragic Hero; besides the human agents in the drama there are the gods, always present in the action, whether assisting or controlling it. To the modern reader not familiar with Greek poetry the gods can be a stumbling-block: they can make him think that the human actors are mere puppets in the hands of Omnipotence. He will come closer to Sophocles' own thought, and consequently to his drama, if he thinks of them as representing rather the immanent laws or conditions of human existence, those which we must obey or perish – in Antigone's case, obey *and* perish. His own actions recoil upon Creon; their own actions recoil upon Clytemnestra and Aegis-thus. In each play Sophocles shows how the recoil happens. Not even are Laius, Iocasta and Oedipus puppets: the idea that shapes this play is that what confronts us – what we call Life – is so vast, so complex, that Man must not arrogantly suppose that he is in control and therefore need no longer respect the restraints of religion. Laius and Oedipus are actually *told* what will befall them; each of them takes control of the situation to dispose of the threat, but for all his resolution and intelligence, neither succeeds – and, within the action of the play, Oedipus' utter reliance on his own judgement leads him to the brink of a tyrannical and stupid crime against Creon.

Taking a hint from the French translators for the Budé series I have here and there added to the lyrical portions a quasi-musical indication of tempo or mood, on no authority except that of common sense. These may at least serve to remind the reader, if he needs reminding, that the lyrics were not recited; they were a fusion of intense poetry, music, and dancing. Of the music we know nothing; of the dance we can at least infer that its range extended from grave processional movements to the expression of great excitement, whether of joy or despair. I have said a little about these rhythms in a short Note at the end of the book. Those who are not interested are recommended not to read it.

I owe the translation of *Electra* 624–5 (611–12 in my version) to John Milton.

CONTENTS

ANTIGONE

DRAMATIS PERSONAE

ANTIGONE, *daughter of Oedipus and Iocasta*
ISMENE, *her sister*
CREON, *King of Thebes, brother of Iocasta*
HAEMON, *his son*
A GUARD
TEIRESIAS, *a Seer*
MESSENGER *or messengers**
EURYDICE, *wife to Creon*
Chorus of Theban nobles

Scene: Thebes, before the royal palace

Antigone and Ismene are the last members of a royal line which stretched back, through Oedipus and Laius, to Cadmus who had founded the city by sowing the Dragon's teeth from which sprang its warrior-race.

The play was first produced, in Athens, in 442 or 441 B.C., when Sophocles was about fifty-five years old. There is an ancient story that the Athenians were so much impressed with the play that in 440 they elected Sophocles one of the ten Generals. The election is certain; the reason alleged may well be a random guess; Sophocles was in any case an experienced man of affairs.

---

* There is not the slightest indication in the text whether the messenger who brings the news of Eurydice's death is a man or a woman. Presumably Sophocles used the same man who had brought the news from the cavern, but it is a matter of complete indifference.

ANTIGONE

Enter, from the palace, ANTIGONE *and* ISMENE

ANTIGONE. Ismene, my own sister, dear Ismene,
How many miseries our father caused!
And is there one of them that does not fall
On us while yet we live? Unhappiness,
Calamity, disgrace, dishonour – which
Of these have you and I not known? And now
Again: there is the order which they say
Brave Creon has proclaimed to all the city.
You understand? or do you not yet know
What outrage threatens one of those we love?   10

ISMENE. Of them, Antigone, I have not heard
Good news or bad – nothing, since we two sisters
Were robbed of our two brothers on one day
When each destroyed the other. During the night
The enemy has fled: so much I know,
But nothing more, either for grief or joy.

ANTIGONE. I knew it; therefore I have brought you here,
Outside the doors, to tell you secretly.

ISMENE. What is it? Some dark shadow is upon you.

ANTIGONE. Our brothers' burial. – Creon has ordained   20
Honour for one, dishonour for the other.
Eteocles, they say, has been entombed
With every solemn rite and ceremony
To do him honour in the world below;
But as for Polyneices, Creon has ordered
That none shall bury him or mourn for him;
He must be left to lie unwept, unburied,
For hungry birds of prey to swoop and feast

3

On his poor body. So he has decreed,
Our noble Creon, to all the citizens:
To you, to me. To me! And he is coming
To make it public here, that no one may
Be left in ignorance; nor does he hold it
Of little moment: he who disobeys
In any detail shall be put to death
By public stoning in the streets of Thebes.
So it is now for you to show if you
Are worthy, or unworthy, of your birth.

ISMENE. O my poor sister! If it has come to this
What can I do, either to help or hinder?

ANTIGONE. Will you join hands with me and share my task?

ISMENE. What dangerous enterprise have you in mind?

ANTIGONE. Will you join me in taking up the body?

ISMENE. What? Would you bury him, against the law?

ANTIGONE. No one shall say *I* failed him! I will bury
My brother – and yours too, if you will not.

ISMENE. You reckless girl! When Creon has forbidden?

ANTIGONE. He has no right to keep me from my own!

ISMENE. Think of our father, dear Antigone,
And how we saw him die, hated and scorned,
When his own hands had blinded his own eyes
Because of sins which he himself disclosed;
And how his mother-wife, two names in one,
Knotted a rope, and so destroyed herself.
And, last of all, upon a single day
Our brothers fought each other to the death
And shed upon the ground the blood that joined them.
Now you and I are left, alone; and think:
If we defy the King's prerogative
And break the law, our death will be more shameful

30

40

50

60

4

Even than theirs. Remember too that we
Are women, not made to fight with men. Since they
Who rule us now are stronger far than we,
In this and worse than this we must obey them.
Therefore, beseeching pardon from the dead,
Since what I do is done on hard compulsion,
I yield to those who have authority;
For useless meddling has no sense at all.

ANTIGONE. I will not urge you. Even if you should wish
To give your help I would not take it now.
Your choice is made. But I shall bury him.
And if I have to die for this pure crime,
I am content, for I shall rest beside him;
His love will answer mine. I have to please
The dead far longer than I need to please
The living; with them, I have to dwell for ever.
But you, if so you choose, you may dishonour
The sacred laws that Heaven holds in honour.

ISMENE. I do them no dishonour, but to act
Against the city's will I am too weak.

ANTIGONE. Make that your pretext! I will go and heap
The earth upon the brother whom I love.

ISMENE. You reckless girl! I tremble for your life.

ANTIGONE. Look to yourself and do not fear for me.

ISMENE. At least let no one hear of it, but keep
Your purpose secret, and so too will I.

ANTIGONE. Go and denounce me! I shall hate you more
If you keep silent and do not proclaim it.

ISMENE. Your heart is hot upon a wintry work!

ANTIGONE. I know I please whom most I ought to please.

ISMENE. But can you do it? It is impossible!

ANTIGONE. When I can do no more, then I will stop.

5

ISMENE. But why attempt a hopeless task at all?

ANTIGONE. O stop, or I shall hate you! He will hate
You too, for ever, justly. Let me be,
Me and my folly! I will face the danger
That so dismays you, for it cannot be
So dreadful as to die a coward's death.

ISMENE. Then go and do it, if you must. It is
Blind folly – but those who love you love you dearly.   100

[*Exeunt severally*

FIRST ODE

Strophe 1

CHORUS. Welcome, light of the Sun, the fairest
(*glyconics*) Sun that ever has dawned upon
Thebes, the city of seven gates!
At last thou art arisen, great
Orb of shining day, pouring
Light across the gleaming water of Dirkê.
Thou hast turned into headlong flight,
Galloping faster and faster, the foe who
Bearing a snow-white shield in full
Panoply came from Argos.   110

(*anapaests*) He had come to destroy us, in Polyneices'
Fierce quarrel. *He* brought them against our land;
And like some eagle screaming his rage
From the sky he descended upon us,
With his armour about him, shining like snow,
    With spear upon spear,
And with plumes that swayed on their helmets.

Antistrophe 1

(*glyconics*) Close he hovered above our houses,
    Circling around our seven gates, with

6

Spears that thirsted to drink our blood.   120
He's gone! gone before ever his jaws
Snapped on our flesh, before he sated
Himself with our blood, before his blazing fire-brand
Seized with its fire our city's towers.
Terrible clangour of arms repelled him,
Driving him back, for hard it is to
Strive with the sons of a Dragon.

(anapaests) For the arrogant boast of an impious man
    Zeus hateth exceedingly. So, when he saw
    This army advancing in swollen flood   130
    In the pride of its gilded equipment,
    He struck them down from the rampart's edge
        With a fiery bolt
    In the midst of their shout of 'Triumph!'

Strophe 2

(more strongly-marked rhythm) Heavily down to the earth did he
                                         fall, and lie there,
    He who with torch in his hand and possessed with frenzy
        Breathed forth bitterest hate
        Like some fierce tempestuous wind.
            So it fared then with him;
    And of the rest, each met his own terrible doom,   140
    Given by the great War-god, our deliverer.

(anapaests) Seven foemen appointed to our seven gates
    Each fell to a Theban, and Argive arms
    Shall grace our Theban temple of Zeus:
    Save two, those two of unnatural hate,
    Two sons of one mother, two sons of one King;
    They strove for the crown, and shared with the sword
    Their estate, each slain by his brother.

7

Antistrophe 2

Yet do we see in our midst, and acclaim with gladness,
Victory, glorious Victory, smiling, welcome.   150
   Now, since danger is past,
    Thoughts of war shall pass from our minds.
     Come! let all thank the gods,
Dancing before temple and shrine all through the night,
Following Thee, Theban Dionysus.

CHORUS-LEADER. But here comes Creon, the new king of Thebes,
   In these new fortunes that the gods have given us.
   What purpose is he furthering, that he
   Has called this gathering of his Counsellors?

Enter CREON, *attended*

CREON. My lords: for what concerns the state, the gods   160
   Who tossed it on the angry surge of strife
   Have righted it again; and therefore you
   By royal edict I have summoned here,
   Chosen from all our number. I know well
   How you revered the throne of Laius;
   And then, when Oedipus maintained our state,
   And when he perished, round his sons you rallied,
   Still firm and steadfast in your loyalty.
   Since they have fallen by a double doom
   Upon a single day, two brothers each   170
   Killing the other with polluted sword,
   I now possess the throne and royal power
   By right of nearest kinship with the dead.
    There is no art that teaches us to know
   The temper, mind or spirit of any man
   Until he has been proved by government
   And lawgiving. A man who rules a state
   And will not ever steer the wisest course,
   But is afraid, and says not what he thinks,
   That man is worthless; and if any holds   180

8

A friend of more account than his own city,
I scorn him; for if I should see destruction
Threatening the safety of my citizens,
I would not hold my peace, nor would I count
That man my friend who was my country's foe,
Zeus be my witness. For be sure of this:
It is the city that protects us all;
She bears us through the storm; only when she
Rides safe and sound can we make loyal friends.

    This I believe, and thus will I maintain   190
Our city's greatness. – Now, conformably,
Of Oedipus' two sons I have proclaimed
This edict: he who in his country's cause
Fought gloriously and so laid down his life,
Shall be entombed and graced with every rite
That men can pay to those who die with honour;
But for his brother, him called Polyneices,
Who came from exile to lay waste his land,
To burn the temples of his native gods,
To drink his kindred blood, and to enslave   200
The rest, I have proclaimed to Thebes that none
Shall give him funeral honours or lament him,
But leave him there unburied, to be devoured
By dogs and birds, mangled most hideously.
Such is my will; never shall I allow
The villain to win more honour than the upright;
But any who show love to this our city
In life and death alike shall win my praise.

CHORUS-LEADER. Such is your will, my lord; so you requite
    Our city's champion and our city's foe.   210
    You, being sovereign, make what laws you will
    Both for the dead and those of us who live.

CREON. See then that you defend the law now made.

CHORUS-LEADER. No, lay that burden on some younger men.

CREON. I have appointed guards to watch the body.

9

CHORUS-LEADER. What further charge, then, do you lay on us?

CREON. Not to connive at those that disobey me.

CHORUS-LEADER. None are so foolish as to long for death.

CREON. Death is indeed the price, but love of gain
    Has often lured a man to his destruction.   220

Enter a GUARD

GUARD. My lord: I cannot say that I am come
    All out of breath with running. More than once
    I stopped and thought and turned round in my path
    And started to go back. My mind had much
    To say to me. One time it said 'You fool!
    Why do you go to certain punishment?'
    Another time 'What? Standing still, you wretch?
    You'll smart for it, if Creon comes to hear
    From someone else.' And so I went along
    Debating with myself, not swift nor sure.   230
    This way, a short road soon becomes a long one.
    At last this was the verdict: I must come
    And tell you. It may be worse than nothing; still,
    I'll tell you. I can suffer nothing more
    Than what is in my fate. There is my comfort!

CREON. And what is this that makes you so despondent?

GUARD. First for myself: I did not see it done,
    I do not know who did it. Plainly then,
    I cannot rightly come to any harm.

CREON. You are a cautious fellow, building up   240
    This barricade. You bring unpleasant news?

GUARD. I do, and peril makes a man pause long.

CREON. O, won't you tell your story and be gone?

GUARD. Then, here it is. The body: someone has
    Just buried it, and gone away. He sprinkled
    Dry dust on it, with all the sacred rites.

CREON. What? Buried it? What man has so defied me?

GUARD. How can I tell? There was no mark of pickaxe,
No sign of digging; the earth was hard and dry
And undisturbed; no waggon had been there;   250
He who had done it left no trace at all.
So, when the first day-watchman showed it to us,
We were appalled. We could not see the body;
It was not buried but was thinly covered
With dust, as if by someone who had sought
To avoid a curse. Although we looked, we saw
No sign that any dog or bird had come
And torn the body. Angry accusations
Flew up between us; each man blamed another,
And in the end it would have come to blows,   260
For there was none to stop it. Each single man
Seemed guilty, yet proclaimed his ignorance
And could not be convicted. We were all
Ready to take hot iron in our hands,
To walk through fire, to swear by all the gods
We had not done it, nor had secret knowledge
Of any man who did it or contrived it.
We could not find a clue. Then one man spoke:
It made us hang our heads in terror, yet
No one could answer him, nor could we see   270
Much profit for ourselves if we should do it.
He said 'We must report this thing to Creon;
We dare not hide it'; and his word prevailed.
I am the unlucky man who drew the prize
When we cast lots, and therefore I am come
Unwilling and, for certain, most unwelcome:
Nobody loves the bringer of bad news.

CHORUS-LEADER. My lord, the thought has risen in my mind:
Do we not see in this the hand of God?

CREON. Silence! or you will anger me. You are   280
An old man: must you be a fool as well?

Intolerable, that you suppose the gods
Should have a single thought for this dead body.
What? should they honour him with burial
As one who served them well, when he had come
To burn their pillared temples, to destroy
Their treasuries, to devastate their land
And overturn its laws? Or have you noticed
The gods prefer the vile? No, from the first
There was a muttering against my edict,   290
Wagging of heads in secret, restiveness
And discontent with my authority.
I know that some of these perverted others
And bribed them to this act. Of all vile things
Current on earth, none is so vile as money.
For money opens wide the city-gates
To ravishers, it drives the citizens
To exile, it perverts the honest mind
To shamefulness, it teaches men to practise
All forms of wickedness and impiety.   300
These criminals who sold themselves for money
Have bought with it their certain punishment;
For, as I reverence the throne of Zeus,
I tell you plainly, and confirm it with
My oath: unless you find, and bring before me,
The very author of this burial-rite
Mere death shall not suffice; you shall be hanged
Alive, until you have disclosed the crime,
That for the future you may ply your trade
More cleverly, and learn not every pocket   310
Is safely to be picked. Ill-gotten gains
More often lead to ruin than to safety.

GUARD. May I reply? Or must I turn and go?

CREON. Now, as before, your very voice offends me.

GUARD. Is it your ears that feel it, or your mind?

CREON. Why must you probe the seat of our displeasure?

12

GUARD. The rebel hurts your mind; I but your ears.

CREON. No more of this! You are a babbling fool!

GUARD. If so, I cannot be the one who did it.

CREON. Yes, but you did – selling your life for money!   320

GUARD. It's bad, to judge at random, and judge wrong!

CREON. You judge my judgement as you will – but bring
    The man who did it, or you shall proclaim
    What punishment is earned by crooked dealings.

GUARD. God grant he may be found! But whether he
    Be found or not – for this must lie with chance –
    You will not see me coming *here* again.
    Alive beyond my hope and expectation,
    I thank the gods who have delivered me.

                  [*Exeunt severally* CREON *and* GUARD

SECOND ODE
Strophe 1

CHORUS. Wonders are many, yet of all   330
(glyconics) Things is Man the most wonderful.
    He can sail on the stormy sea
    Though the tempest rage, and the loud
    Waves roar around, as he makes his
    Path amid the towering surge.

(dactyls) Earth inexhaustible, ageless, he wearies, as
    Backwards and forwards, from season to season, his
    Ox-team drives along the ploughshare.

Antistrophe 1

    He can entrap the cheerful birds,   340
    Setting a snare, and all the wild
    Beasts of the earth he has learned to catch, and

Fish that teem in the deep sea, with
Nets knotted of stout cords; of
Such inventiveness is man.
Through his inventions he becomes lord
Even of the beasts of the mountain: the long-haired
Horse he subdues to the yoke on his neck, and the
Hill-bred bull, of strength untiring.

Strophe 2

And speech he has learned, and thought   350
So swift, and the temper of mind
To dwell within cities, and not to lie bare
Amid the keen, biting frosts
Or cower beneath pelting rain;
Full of resource against all that comes to him
Is Man. Against Death alone
He is left with no defence.
But painful sickness he can cure
        By his own skill.

Antistrophe 2

Surpassing belief, the device and   360
Cunning that Man has attained,
And it bringeth him now to evil, now to good.
If he observe Law, and tread
The righteous path God ordained,
Honoured is he; dishonoured, the man whose reckless heart
Shall make him join hands with sin:
May I not think like him,
Nor may such an impious man
        Dwell in my house.

Enter GUARD, *with* ANTIGONE

CHORUS-LEADER. What evil spirit is abroad? I know   370
    Her well: Antigone. But how can I
    Believe it? Why, O you unlucky daughter

14

Of an unlucky father, what is this?
Can it be you, so mad and so defiant,
So disobedient to a King's decree?

GUARD. Here is the one who did the deed, this girl;
We caught her burying him. – But where is Creon?

CHORUS-LEADER. He comes, just as you need him, from the palace.

Enter CREON, *attended*

CREON. How? What occasion makes my coming timely?

GUARD. Sir, against nothing should a man take oath,   380
For second thoughts belie him. Under your threats
That lashed me like a hailstorm, I'd have said
I would not quickly have come here again;
But joy that comes beyond our dearest hope
Surpasses all in magnitude. So I
Return, though I had sworn I never would,
Bringing this girl detected in the act
Of honouring the body. This time no lot
Was cast; the windfall is my very own.
And so, my lord, do as you please: take her   390
Yourself, examine her, cross-question her.
I claim the right of free and final quittance.

CREON. Why do you bring this girl? Where was she taken?

GUARD. In burying the body. That is all.

CREON. You know what you are saying? Do you mean it?

GUARD. I saw her giving burial to the corpse
You had forbidden. Is that plain and clear?

CREON. How did you see and take her so red-handed?

GUARD. It was like this. When we had reached the place,
Those dreadful threats of yours upon our heads,   400
We swept aside each grain of dust that hid
The clammy body, leaving it quite bare,
And sat down on a hill, to the windward side

15

That so we might avoid the smell of it.
We kept sharp look-out; each man roundly cursed
His neighbour, if he should neglect his duty.
So the time passed, until the blazing sun
Reached his mid-course and burned us with his heat.
Then, suddenly, a whirlwind came from heaven
And raised a storm of dust, which blotted out   410
The earth and sky; the air was filled with sand
And leaves ripped from the trees. We closed our eyes
And bore this visitation as we could.
At last it ended; then we saw the girl.
She raised a bitter cry, as will a bird
Returning to its nest and finding it
Despoiled, a cradle empty of its young.
So, when she saw the body bare, she raised
A cry of anguish mixed with imprecations
Laid upon those who did it; then at once   420
Brought handfuls of dry dust, and raised aloft
A shapely vase of bronze, and three times poured
The funeral libation for the dead.
We rushed upon her swiftly, seized our prey,
And charged her both with this offence and that.
She faced us calmly; she did not disown
The double crime. How glad I was! – and yet
How sorry too; it is a painful thing
To bring a friend to ruin. Still, for me,
My own escape comes before everything.   430

CREON. You there, who keep your eyes fixed on the ground,
  Do you admit this, or do you deny it?

ANTIGONE. No, I do not deny it. I admit it.

CREON [*to Guard*]. Then you may go; go where you like. You
                      have
  Been fully cleared of that grave accusation.

                           [*Exit* GUARD

  You: tell me briefly – I want no long speech:
  Did you not know that this had been forbidden?

ANTIGONE. Of course I knew. There was a proclamation.

CREON. And so you dared to disobey the law?

ANTIGONE. It was not Zeus who published this decree,   440
   Nor have the Powers who rule among the dead
   Imposed such laws as this upon mankind;
   Nor could I think that a decree of yours –
   A man – could override the laws of Heaven
   Unwritten and unchanging. Not of today
   Or yesterday is their authority;
   They are eternal; no man saw their birth.
   Was I to stand before the gods' tribunal
   For disobeying *them*, because I feared
   A man? I knew that I should have to die,   450
   Even without your edict; if I die
   Before my time, why then, I count it gain;
   To one who lives as I do, ringed about
   With countless miseries, why, death is welcome.
   For me to meet this doom is little grief;
   But when my mother's son lay dead, had I
   Neglected him and left him there unburied,
   That would have caused me grief; this causes none.
   And if you think it folly, then perhaps
   I am accused of folly by the fool.   460

CHORUS-LEADER. The daughter shows her father's temper – fierce,
   Defiant; she will not yield to any storm.

CREON. But it is those that are most obstinate
   Suffer the greatest fall; the hardest iron,
   Most fiercely tempered in the fire, that is
   Most often snapped and splintered. I have seen
   The wildest horses tamed, and only by
   The tiny bit. There is no room for pride
   In one who is a slave! This girl already
   Had fully learned the art of insolence   470
   When she transgressed the laws that I established;
   And now to that she adds a second outrage –

To boast of what she did, and laugh at us.
Now she would be the man, not I, if she
Defeated me and did not pay for it.
But though she be my niece, or closer still
Than all our family, she shall not escape
The direst penalty; no, nor shall her sister:
I judge her guilty too; she played her part
In burying the body. Summon her.   480
Just now I saw her raving and distracted
Within the palace. So it often is:
Those who plan crime in secret are betrayed
Despite themselves; they show it in their faces.
But this is worst of all: to be convicted
And then to glorify the crime as virtue.

                                 [*Exeunt some* GUARDS

ANTIGONE. Would you do more than simply take and kill me?

CREON. I will have nothing more, and nothing less.

ANTIGONE. Then why delay? To me no word of yours
Is pleasing – God forbid it should be so! –   490
And everything in me displeases you.
Yet what could I have done to win renown
More glorious than giving burial
To my own brother? These men too would say it,
Except that terror cows them into silence.
A king has many a privilege: the greatest,
That he can say and do all that he will.

CREON. You are the only one in Thebes to think it!

ANTIGONE. These think as I do – but they dare not speak.

CREON. Have you no shame, not to conform with others?   500

ANTIGONE. To reverence a brother is no shame.

CREON. Was he no brother, he who died for Thebes?

ANTIGONE. One mother and one father gave them birth.

CREON. Honouring the traitor, you dishonour *him*.

18

ANTIGONE. He will not bear this testimony, in death.

CREON. Yes! if the traitor fare the same as he.

ANTIGONE. It was a brother, not a slave who died!

CREON. He died attacking Thebes; the other saved us.

ANTIGONE. Even so, the god of Death demands these rites.

CREON. The good demand more honour than the wicked.   510

ANTIGONE. Who knows? In death they may be reconciled.

CREON. Death does not make an enemy a friend!

ANTIGONE. Even so, I give both love, not share their hatred.

CREON. Down then to Hell! Love there, if love you must.
    While I am living, no woman shall have rule.

Enter GUARDS, *with* ISMENE

CHORUS-LEADER. See where Ismene leaves the palace-gate,
    In tears shed for her sister. On her brow
    A cloud of grief has blotted out her sun,
    And breaks in rain upon her comeliness.

CREON. You, lurking like a serpent in my house,   520
    Drinking my life-blood unawares; nor did
    I know that I was cherishing two fiends,
    Subverters of my throne: come, tell me this:
    Do you confess you shared this burial,
    Or will you swear you had no knowledge of it?

ISMENE. I did it too, if she allows my claim;
    I share the burden of this heavy charge.

ANTIGONE. No! Justice will not suffer that; for you
    Refused, and I gave you no part in it.

ISMENE. But in your stormy voyage I am glad   530
    To share the danger, travelling at your side.

ANTIGONE. Whose was the deed the god of Death knows well;
I love not those who love in words alone.

ISMENE. My sister, do not scorn me, nor refuse
That I may die with you, honouring the dead.

ANTIGONE. You shall not die with me, nor claim as yours
What you rejected. My death will be enough.

ISMENE. What life is left to me if I lose you?

ANTIGONE. Ask Creon! It was Creon that you cared for.

ISMENE. O why taunt me, when it does not help you?   540

ANTIGONE. If I do taunt you, it is to my pain.

ISMENE. Can I not help you, even at this late hour?

ANTIGONE. Save your own life. I grudge not your escape.

ISMENE. Alas! Can I not join you in your fate?

ANTIGONE. You cannot: you chose life, and I chose death.

ISMENE. But not without the warning that I gave you!

ANTIGONE. Some thought *you* wise; the dead commended me.

ISMENE. But my offence has been as great as yours.

ANTIGONE. Be comforted; you live, but I have given
My life already, in service of the dead.   550

CREON. Of these two girls, one has been driven frantic,
The other has been frantic since her birth.

ISMENE. Not so, my lord; but when disaster comes
The reason that one has can not stand firm.

CREON. Yours did not, when you chose to partner crime!

ISMENE. But what is life to me, without my sister?

CREON. Say not 'my sister': sister you have none.

ISMENE. But she is Haemon's bride – and can you kill her?

CREON. Is she the only woman he can bed with?

ISMENE. The only one so joined in love with him.   560

CREON. I hate a son to have an evil wife.

ANTIGONE. O my dear Haemon! How your father wrongs you!

CREON. I hear too much of you and of your marriage.

ISMENE. He is your son; how can you take her from him?

CREON. It is not I, but Death, that stops this wedding.

CHORUS-LEADER. It is determined, then, that she must die?

CREON. For you, and me, determined. [To the GUARDS.] Take
                                         them in
At once; no more delay. Henceforward let
Them stay at home, like women, not roam abroad.
Even the bold, you know, will seek escape   570
When they see death at last standing beside them.

> [Exeunt ANTIGONE and ISMENE into the palace,
> guarded. CREON remains

THIRD ODE

Strophe 1

CHORUS. Thrice happy are they who have never known disaster!
Once a house is shaken of Heaven, disaster
Never leaves it, from generation to generation.
'Tis even as the swelling sea,
When the roaring wind from Thrace
Drives blustering over the water and makes it black:
It bears up from below
A thick, dark cloud of mud,
And groaning cliffs repel the smack of wind and angry   580
                                         breakers.

21

Antistrophe 1

I see, in the house of our kings, how ancient sorrows
Rise again; disaster is linked with disaster.
Woe again must each generation inherit. Some god
   Besets them, nor will give release.
   On the last of royal blood
There gleamed a shimmering light in the house of Oedipus.
   But Death comes once again
   With blood-stained axe, and hews
The sapling down; and Frenzy lends her aid, and vengeful
                                    Madness.

Strophe 2

   Thy power, Zeus, is almighty! No   590
   Mortal insolence can oppose Thee!
Sleep, which conquers all else, cannot overcome Thee,
   Nor can the never-wearied
   Years, but throughout
   Time Thou art strong and ageless,
     In thy own Olympus
   Ruling in radiant splendour.
   For today, and in all past time,
   And through all time to come,
   This is the law: that in Man's   600
Life every success brings with it some disaster.

Antistrophe 2

   Hope springs high, and to many a man
   Hope brings comfort and consolation;
Yet she is to some nothing but fond illusion:
   Swiftly they come to ruin,
   As when a man
   Treads unawares on hot fire.
    For it was a wise man
   First made that ancient saying:

22

To the man whom God will ruin   610
　　One day shall evil seem
　　Good, in his twisted judgement
He comes in a short time to fell disaster.

CHORUS-LEADER. See, here comes Haemon, last-born of your
　　　　　　　　　　　　　　　　　　　　children,
　　Grieving, it may be, for Antigone.

CREON. Soon we shall know, better than seers can tell us.

Enter HAEMON

My son:
You have not come in rage against your father
Because your bride must die? Or are you still
My loyal son, whatever I may do?   620

HAEMON. Father, I am your son; may your wise judgement
　　Rule me, and may I always follow it.
　　No marriage shall be thought a greater prize
　　For me to win than your good government.

CREON. So may you ever be resolved, my son,
　　In all things to be guided by your father.
　　It is for this men pray that they may have
　　Obedient children, that they may requite
　　Their father's enemy with enmity
　　And honour whom their father loves to honour.   630
　　One who begets unprofitable children
　　Makes trouble for himself, and gives his foes
　　Nothing but laughter. Therefore do not let
　　Your pleasure in a woman overcome
　　Your judgement, knowing this, that if you have
　　An evil wife to share your house, you'll find
　　Cold comfort in your bed. What other wound
　　Can cut so deep as treachery at home?
　　So, think this girl your enemy; spit on her,
　　And let her find her husband down in Hell!   640
　　She is the only one that I have found
23

In all the city disobedient.
I will not make myself a liar. I
Have caught her; I will kill her. Let her sing
Her hymns to Sacred Kinship! If I breed
Rebellion in the house, then it is certain
There'll be no lack of rebels out of doors.
No man can rule a city uprightly
Who is not just in ruling his own household.
Never will I approve of one who breaks   650
And violates the law, or would dictate
To those who rule. Lawful authority
Must be obeyed in all things, great or small,
Just and unjust alike; and such a man
Would win my confidence both in command
And as a subject; standing at my side
In the storm of battle he would hold his ground,
Not leave me unprotected. But there is
No greater curse than disobedience.
This brings destruction on a city, this   660
Drives men from hearth and home, this brings about
A sudden panic in the battle-front.
Where all goes well, obedience is the cause.
So we must vindicate the law; we must not be
Defeated by a woman. Better far
Be overthrown, if need be, by a man
Than to be called the victim of a woman.

CHORUS-LEADER. Unless the years have stolen away our wits,
    All you say is said most prudently.

HAEMON. Father, it is the gods who give us wisdom;   670
    No gift of theirs more precious. I cannot say
    That you are wrong, nor would I ever learn
    That impudence, although perhaps another
    Might fairly say it. But it falls to me,
    Being your son, to note what others say,
    Or do, or censure in you, for your glance
    Intimidates the common citizen;

He will not say, before your face, what might
Displease you; I can listen freely, how
The city mourns this girl. 'No other woman',   680
So they are saying, 'so undeservedly
Has been condemned for such a glorious deed.
When her own brother had been slain in battle
She would not let his body lie unburied
To be devoured by dogs or birds of prey.
Is not this worthy of a crown of gold?' –
Such is the muttering that spreads everywhere.

    Father, no greater treasure can I have
Than your prosperity; no son can find
A greater prize than his own father's fame,   690
No father than his son's. Therefore let not
This single thought possess you: only what
You say is right, and nothing else. The man
Who thinks that he alone is wise, that he
Is best in speech or counsel, such a man
Brought to the proof is found but emptiness.
There's no disgrace, even if one is wise,
In learning more, and knowing when to yield.
See how the trees that grow beside a torrent
Preserve their branches, if they bend; the others,   700
Those that resist, are torn out, root and branch.
So too the captain of a ship; let him
Refuse to shorten sail, despite the storm –
He'll end his voyage bottom uppermost.
No, let your anger cool, and be persuaded.
If one who is still young can speak with sense,
Then I would say that he does best who has
Most understanding; second best, the man
Who profits from the wisdom of another.

CHORUS-LEADER. My lord, he has not spoken foolishly;   710
    You each can learn some wisdom from the other.

CREON. What? men of our age go to school again
    And take a lesson from a very boy?

HAEMON. If it is worth the taking. I am young,
But think what should be done, not of my age.

CREON. What should be done! To honour disobedience!

HAEMON. I would not have you honour criminals.

CREON. And is this girl then not a criminal?

HAEMON. The city with a single voice denies it.

CREON. Must I give orders then by their permission?   720

HAEMON. If youth is folly, this is childishness.

CREON. Am I to rule for them, not for myself?

HAEMON. That is not government, but tyranny.

CREON. The king is lord and master of his city.

HAEMON. Then you had better rule a desert island!

CREON. This man, it seems, is the ally of the woman.

HAEMON. If you're the woman, yes! I fight for you.

CREON. Villain! Do you oppose your father's will?

HAEMON. Only because you are opposing Justice.

CREON. When I regard my own prerogative?   730

HAEMON. Opposing God's, you disregard your own.

CREON. Scoundrel, so to surrender to a woman!

HAEMON. But not to anything that brings me shame.

CREON. Your every word is in defence of her.

HAEMON. And me, and you – and of the gods below.

CREON. You shall not marry her this side the grave!

HAEMON. So, she must die – and will not die alone.

CREON. What? Threaten me? Are you so insolent?

26

HAEMON. It is no threat, if I reply to folly.

CREON. The fool would teach me sense! You'll pay for it.   740

HAEMON. I'd call you mad, if you were not my father.

CREON. I'll hear no chatter from a woman's plaything.

HAEMON. Would you have all the talk, and hear no answer?

CREON. So?
  I swear to God, you shall not bandy words
  With me and not repent it! Bring her out,
  That loathsome creature! I will have her killed
  At once, before her bridegroom's very eyes.

HAEMON. How can you think it? I will not see that,
  Nor shall you ever see my face again.   750
  Those friends of yours who can must tolerate
  Your raging madness; I will not endure it.

  [*Exit* HAEMON

CHORUS-LEADER. How angrily he went, my lord! The young,
  When they are greatly hurt, grow desperate.

CREON. Then let his pride and folly do their worst!
  He shall not save these women from their doom.

CHORUS-LEADER. Is it your purpose then to kill them both?

CREON. Not her who had no part in it. – I thank you.

CHORUS-LEADER. And for the other: how is she to die?

CREON. I'll find a cave in some deserted spot,   760
  And there I will imprison her alive
  With so much food – no more – as will avert
  Pollution and a curse upon the city.
  There let her pray to Death, the only god
  Whom she reveres, to rescue her from death,
  Or learn at last, though it be late, that it
  Is wanton folly to respect the dead.
                    [CREON *remains on the stage*

FOURTH ODE
Strophe

CHORUS. Invincible, implacable Love, O
   Love, that makes havoc of all wealth;
   That peacefully keeps his night-watch   770
   On tender cheek of a maiden:
   The Sea is no barrier, nor
   Mountainous waste to Love's flight; for
   No one can escape Love's domination,
   Man, no, nor immortal god. Love's
   Prey is possessed by madness.

Antistrophe

   By Love, the mind even of the just
   Is bent awry; he becomes unjust.
   So here: it is Love that stirred up
   This quarrel of son with father.   780
   The kindling light of Love in the soft
   Eye of a bride conquers, for
   Love sits on his throne, one of the great Powers;
   Nought else can prevail against
   Invincible Aphrodite.

Enter ANTIGONE, *under guard. (From this point up to the end of the
fifth ode everything is sung, except the two speeches in blank verse.)*

CHORUS.   I too, when I see this sight, cannot stay
(anapaests) Within bounds; I cannot keep back my tears
   Which rise like a flood. For behold, they bring
   Antigone here, on the journey that all
   Must make, to the silence of Hades.   790

COMMOS
Strophe 1

ANTIGONE. Behold me, O lords of my native city!
(glyconics) Now do I make my last journey;

Now do I see the last
Sun that ever I shall behold.
Never another! Death, that lulls
All to sleep, takes me while I live
Down to the grim shore of Acheron.
No wedding day can be
Mine, no hymn will be raised to honour
Marriage of mine; for I   800
Go to espouse the bridegroom, Death.

CHORUS.   Yet a glorious death, and rich in fame
(anapaests) Is yours; you go to the silent tomb
Not smitten with wasting sickness, nor
Repaying a debt to the sharp-edged sword;
But alone among mortals you go to the home
Of the dead while yet you are living.

Antistrophe 1

ANTIGONE. They tell of how cruelly she did perish,
(glyconics) Niobe, Queen in Thebes;
For, as ivy grows on a tree,   810
Strangling it, so she slowly turned to
Stone on a Phrygian mountain-top.
Now the rain-storms wear her away –
So does the story run – and
Snow clings to her always:
Tears fall from her weeping eyes for
Ever and ever. Like to hers, the
Cruel death that now awaits me.

CHORUS.   But she was a goddess, and born of the gods;
(anapaests) We are but mortals, of mortals born.   820
For a mortal to share in the doom of a god,
That brings her renown while yet she lives,
And a glory that long will outlive her.

29

Strophe 2

ANTIGONE. Alas, they laugh! O by the gods of Thebes, my

(more passionate rhythm) native city,

    Mock me, if you must, when I am gone, not to my face!

    O Thebes my city, O you lordly men of Thebes!

    O water of Dirkê's stream! Holy soil where our chariots run!

    You, you do I call upon; you, you shall testify

    How all unwept of friends, by what harsh decree,

    They send me to the cavern that shall be my everlasting

                          grave. 830

    Ah, cruel doom! to be banished from earth, nor welcomed

    Among the dead, set apart, for ever!

CHORUS. Too bold, too reckless, you affronted

(more spirited) Justice. Now that awful power

    Takes terrible vengeance, O my child.

    For some old sin you make atonement.

Antistrophe 2

ANTIGONE. My father's sin! There is the source of all my anguish.

    Harsh fate that befell my father! Harsh fate that has held

    Fast in its grip the whole renowned race of Labdacus!

    O the blind madness of my father's and my mother's

                        marriage! 840

    O cursed union of a son with his own mother!

    From such as those I draw my own unhappy life;

    And now I go to dwell with them, unwedded and accursed.

    O brother, through an evil marriage you were slain; and I

    Live – but your dead hand destroys me.

CHORUS. Such loyalty is a holy thing.

    Yet none that holds authority

    Can brook disobedience, O my child.

    Your self-willed pride has been your ruin.

Epode

ANTIGONE. Unwept, unwedded and unbefriended,   850
    Alone, pitilessly used,
    Now they drag me to death.
    Never again, O thou Sun in the heavens,
    May I look on thy holy radiance!
    Such is my fate, and no one laments it;
    No friend is here to mourn me.

CREON. Enough of this! If tears and lamentations
    Could stave off death they would go on for ever.
    Take her away at once, and wall her up
    Inside a cavern, as I have commanded,   860
    And leave her there, alone, in solitude.
    Her home shall be her tomb; there she may live
    Or die, as she may choose: my hands are clean;
    But she shall live no more among the living.

ANTIGONE. O grave, my bridal-chamber, everlasting
    Prison within a rock: now I must go
    To join my own, those many who have died
    And whom Persephone has welcomed home;
    And now to me, the last of all, so young,
    Death comes, so cruelly. And yet I go   870
    In the sure hope that you will welcome me,
    Father, and you, my mother; you, my brother.
    For when you died it was my hands that washed
    And dressed you, laid you in your graves, and poured
    The last libations. Now, because to you,
    Polyneices, I have given burial,
    To me they give a recompense like this!
    Yet what I did, the wise will all approve.
    For had I lost a son, or lost a husband,
    Never would I have ventured such an act   880
    Against the city's will. And wherefore so?
    My husband dead, I might have found another;
    Another son from him, if I had lost

A son. But since my mother and my father
Have both gone to the grave, there can be none
Henceforth that I can ever call my brother.
It was for this I paid you such an honour,
Dear Polyneices, and in Creon's eyes
Thus wantonly and gravely have offended.
So with rude hands he drags me to my death.   890
No chanted wedding-hymn, no bridal-joy,
No tender care of children can be mine;
But like an outcast, and without a friend,
They take me to the cavernous home of death.
What ordinance of the gods have I transgressed?
Why should I look to Heaven any more
For help, or seek an ally among men?
If this is what the gods approve, why then,
When I am dead I shall discern my fault;
If theirs the sin, may they endure a doom   900
No worse than mine, so wantonly inflicted!

CHORUS.   Still from the same quarter the same wild winds
(anapaests) Blow fiercely, and shake her stubborn soul.

CREON.   And therefore, for this, these men shall have cause,
(anapaests) Bitter cause, to lament their tardiness.

CHORUS. I fear these words bring us closer yet
            To the verge of death.

CREON. I have nothing to say, no comfort to give:
    The sentence is passed, and the end is here.

ANTIGONE. O city of Thebes where my fathers dwelt,   910
        O gods of our race,
    Now at last their hands are upon me!
    You princes of Thebes, O look upon me,
    The last that remain of a line of kings!
    How savagely impious men use me,
    For keeping a law that is holy.
                    [*Exit* ANTIGONE, *under guard.* CREON *remains*
                32

FIFTH ODE

Strophe 1

CHORUS. There was one in days of old who was imprisoned
(slow three-time) In a chamber like a grave, within a tower:
    Fair Danaë, who in darkness was held, and never saw the pure
                                    daylight.
    Yet she too, O my child, was of an ancient line,   920
    Entrusted with divine seed that had come in shower of gold.
    Mysterious, overmastering, is the power of Fate.
(faster three-time) From this, nor wealth nor force of arms
        Nor strong encircling city-walls
        Nor storm-tossed ship can give deliverance.

Antistrophe 1

    Close bondage was ordained by Dionysus
    For one who in a frenzy had denied
    His godhead: in a cavern Lycurgus, for his sin, was imprisoned.
    In such wise did his madness bear a bitter fruit,
    Which withered in a dungeon. So he learned it was a god   930
    He had ventured in his blindness to revile and taunt.
        The sacred dances he had tried
        To quell, and end the Bacchic rite,
        Offending all the tuneful Muses.

Strophe 2

(fairly fast, becoming faster; three- and four-time mixed) There is
        a town by the rocks where a sea meets another sea,
    Two black rocks by the Bosphorus, near the Thracian coast,
    Salmȳdessus; and there a wife had been spurned,
        Held close in bitter constraint.[1]

---

[1] These two verses are a paraphrase rather than a translation. It seemed better to give the audience something which it could follow rather than the mythological reference in the Greek, which it certainly would not.

Then upon both her children
  A blinding wound fell from her cruel rival: 940
With shuttle in hand she smote the open eyes with sharp
And blood-stained point, and brought to Phineus'
Two sons a darkness that cried for vengeance.

Antistrophe 2

In bitter grief and despair they bewailed their unhappy lot,
Children born to a mother whose marriage proved accursed.
Yet she came of a race of ancient kings,
    Her sire the offspring of gods.
    Reared in a distant country,
  Among her fierce, northern father's tempests,
She went, a Boread, swift as horses, over the lofty   950
Mountains. Yet not even she was
Safe against the long-lived Fates, my daughter.

Enter TEIRESIAS, *led by a boy*

TEIRESIAS. My lords, I share my journey with this boy
  Whose eyes must see for both; for so the blind
  Must move abroad, with one to guide their steps.

CREON. Why, what is this? Why are *you* here, Teiresias?

TEIRESIAS. I will explain; you will do well to listen.

CREON. Have I not always followed your good counsel?

TEIRESIAS. You have; therefore we have been guided well.

CREON. I have had much experience of your wisdom.   960

TEIRESIAS. Then think: once more you tread the razor's edge.

CREON. You make me tremble! What is it you mean?

TEIRESIAS. What divination has revealed to me,
  That I will tell you. To my ancient seat
  Of augury I went, where all the birds
  Foregather. There I sat, and heard a clamour
  Strange and unnatural – birds screaming in rage.
  I knew that they were tearing at each other

34

With murderous claws: the beating of their wings
Meant nothing less than that; and I was frightened. 970
I made a blazing fire upon the altar
And offered sacrifice: it would not burn;
The melting fat oozed out upon the embers
And smoked and bubbled; high into the air
The bladder spirted gall, and from the bones
The fatty meat slid off and left them bare.
Such omens, baffling, indistinct, I learned
From him who guides me, as I am guide to others.
Sickness has come upon us, and the cause
Is you: our altars and our sacred hearths 980
Are all polluted by the dogs and birds
That have been gorging on the fallen body
Of Polyneices. Therefore heaven will not
Accept from us our prayers, no fire will burn
Our offerings, nor will birds give out clear sounds,
For they are glutted with the blood of men.
Be warned, my son. No man alive is free
From error, but the wise and prudent man
When he has fallen into evil courses
Does not persist, but tries to find amendment. 990
It is the stubborn man who is the fool.
Yield to the dead, forbear to strike the fallen;
To slay the slain, is that a deed of valour?
Your good is what I seek; and that instruction
Is best that comes from wisdom, and brings profit.

CREON. Sir, all of you, like bowmen at a target,
    Let fly your shafts at me. Now they have turned
    Even diviners on me! By that tribe
    I am bought and sold and stowed away on board.
    Go, make your profits, drive your trade 1000
    In Lydian silver or in Indian gold,
    But him you shall not bury in a tomb,
    No, not though Zeus' own eagles eat the corpse
    And bear the carrion to their master's throne:

Not even so, for fear of that defilement,
Will I permit his burial – for well I know
That mortal man can not defile the gods.
But, old Teiresias, even the cleverest men
Fall shamefully when for a little money
They use fair words to mask their villainy.   1010

TEIRESIAS. Does any man reflect, does any know . . .

CREON. Know *what*? Why do you preach at me like this?

TEIRESIAS. How much the greatest blessing is good counsel?

CREON. As much, I think, as folly is his plague.

TEIRESIAS. Yet with this plague you are yourself infected.

CREON. I will not bandy words with any prophet.

TEIRESIAS. And yet you say my prophecies are dishonest!

CREON. Prophets have always been too fond of gold.

TEIRESIAS. And tyrants, of the shameful use of power.

CREON. You know it is your King of whom you speak?   1020

TEIRESIAS. King of the land I saved from mortal danger.

CREON. A clever prophet – but an evil one.

TEIRESIAS. You'll rouse me to awaken my dark secret.

CREON. Awaken it, but do not speak for money.

TEIRESIAS. And do you think that I am come to *that*?

CREON. You shall not buy and sell *my* policy.

TEIRESIAS. Then I will tell you this: you will not live
Through many circuits of the racing sun
Before you give a child of your own body
To make amends for murder, death for death;   1030
Because you have thrust down within the earth
One who should walk upon it, and have lodged
A living soul dishonourably in a tomb;

36

And impiously have kept upon the earth
Unburied and unblest one who belongs
Neither to you nor to the upper gods
But to the gods below, who are despoiled
By you. Therefore the gods arouse against you
Their sure avengers; they lie in your path
Even now to trap you and to make you pay   1040
Their price. – Now think: do I say *this* for money?
Not many hours will pass before your house
Rings loud with lamentation, men and women.
Hatred for you is moving in those cities
Whose mangled sons had funeral-rites from dogs
Or from some bird of prey, whose wings have carried
The taint of dead men's flesh to their own homes,
Polluting hearth and altar.
These are the arrows that I launch at you,
Because you anger me. I shall not miss   1050
My aim, and you shall not escape their smart.
Boy, lead me home again, that he may vent
His rage upon some younger man, and learn
To moderate his violent tongue, and find
More understanding than he has today.

[*Exit* TEIRESIAS

CHORUS-LEADER. And so, my lord, he leaves us, with a threat
    Of doom. I have lived long, but I am sure
    Of this: no single prophecy that he
    Has made to Thebes has gone without fulfilment.

CREON. I know it too, and I am terrified.   1060
    To yield is very hard, but to resist
    And meet disaster, that is harder still.

CHORUS-LEADER. Creon, this is no time for wrong decision.

CREON. What shall I do? Advise me; I will listen.

CHORUS-LEADER. Release Antigone from her rock-hewn dungeon,
    And lay the unburied body in a tomb.

37

CREON. Is this your counsel? You would have me yield?

CHORUS-LEADER. I would, and quickly. The destroying hand
Of Heaven is quick to punish human error.

CREON. How hard it is! And yet one cannot fight   1070
Against Necessity. – I will give way.

CHORUS-LEADER. Go then and do it; leave it not to others.

CREON. Just as I am I go. – You men-at-arms,
You here, and those within: away at once
Up to the hill, and take your implements.
Now that my resolution is reversed
I who imprisoned her will set her free. –
    I fear it may be wisest to observe
Throughout one's life the laws that are established.

                             [*Exit* CREON

SIXTH ODE
Strophe 1

CHORUS. Thou Spirit whose names are many, Dionysus,   1080
Born to Zeus the loud-thunderer,
Joy of thy Theban mother-nymph,
Lover of famous Italy:
King art thou in the crowded shrine
Where Demeter has her abode, O
Bacchus! Here is thy mother's home,
Here is thine, by the smooth Is-
mênus' flood, here where the savage
Dragon's teeth had offspring.

Antistrophe 1

Thou art seen by the nymphs amid the smoky torchlight, 1090
Where, upon Parnassus' height,
They hold revels to honour Thee

Close to the spring of Castaly.
Thou art come from the ivy-clad
Slopes of Asian hills, and vineyards
Hanging thick with clustering grapes.
Mystic voices chant: 'O
Bacchus! O Bacchus!' in
The roads and ways of Thebê.

Strophe 2

Here is thy chosen home,   1100
In Thebes above all lands,
With thy mother, bride of Zeus.
Wherefore, since a pollution holds
All our people fast in its grip,
O come with swift healing across the wall of high Parnassus,
Or over the rough Eurîpus.

Antistrophe 2

Stars that move, breathing flame,
Honour Thee as they dance;
Voices cry to Thee in the night.
Son begotten of Zeus, appear!   1110
Come, Lord, with thy company,
Thy own nymphs, who with wild, nightlong dances praise
                                                        Thee,
Bountiful Dionysus!

Enter a MESSENGER

MESSENGER. You noblemen of Thebes, how insecure
Is human fortune! Chance will overthrow
The great, and raise the lowly; nothing's firm,
Either for confidence or for despair;
No one can prophesy what lies in store.
An hour ago, how much I envied Creon!
He had saved Thebes, we had accorded him   1120

39

The sovereign power; he ruled our land
Supported by a noble prince, his son.
Now all is lost, and he who forfeits joy
Forfeits his life; he is a breathing corpse.
Heap treasures in your palace, if you will,
And wear the pomp of royalty; but if
You have no happiness, I would not give
A straw for all of it, compared with joy.

CHORUS-LEADER. What is this weight of heavy news you bring?

MESSENGER. Death! – and the blood-guilt rests upon the
living. 1130

CHORUS-LEADER. Death? Who is dead? And who has killed him?
Tell me.

MESSENGER. Haemon is dead, and by no stranger's hand.

CHORUS-LEADER. But by his father's? Or was it his own?

MESSENGER. His own – inflamed with anger at his father.

CHORUS-LEADER. Yours was no idle prophecy, Teiresias!

MESSENGER. That is my news. What next, remains with you.

CHORUS-LEADER. But look! There is his wife, Eurydice;
She is coming from the palace. Has she heard
About her son, or is she here by chance?

Enter EURYDICE

EURYDICE. You citizens of Thebes, I overheard   1140
When I was standing at the gates, for I
Had come to make an offering at the shrine
Of Pallas, and my hand was on the bar
That holds the gate, to draw it; then there fell
Upon my ears a voice that spoke of death.
My terror took away my strength; I fell
Into my servants' arms and swooned away.
But tell it me once more; I can endure
To listen; I am no stranger to bad news.

40

MESSENGER. Dear lady, I was there, and I will tell
The truth; I will not keep it back from you.
Why should I gloze it over? You would hear
From someone else, and I should seem a liar.
The truth is always best.
                                    I went with Creon
Up to the hill where Polyneices' body
Still lay, unpitied, torn by animals.
We gave it holy washing, and we prayed
To Hecate and Pluto that they would
Restrain their anger and be merciful.
And then we cut some branches, and we burned
What little had been left, and built a mound
Over his ashes of his native soil.
Then, to the cavern, to the home of death,
The bridal-chamber with its bed of stone.
One of us heard a cry of lamentation
From that unhallowed place; he went to Creon
And told him. On the wind, as he came near,
Cries of despair were borne. He groaned aloud
In anguish: 'O, and are my fears come true?
Of all the journeys I have made, am I
To find this one the most calamitous?
It is my son's voice greets me. Hurry, men;
Run to the place, and when you reach the tomb
Creep in between the gaping stones and see
If it be Haemon there, or if the gods
Are cheating me.' Upon this desperate order
We ran and looked. Within the furthest chamber
We saw her hanging, dead; strips from her dress
Had served her for a rope. Haemon we saw
Embracing her dead body and lamenting
His loss, his father's deed, and her destruction.
When Creon saw him he cried out in anguish,
Went in, and called to him: 'My son! my son!
O why? What have you done? What brought you here?
What is this madness? O come out, my son,

41

Come, I implore you!' Haemon glared at him
With anger in his eyes, spat in his face,
Said nothing, drew his double-hilted sword,
But missed his aim as Creon leapt aside.
Then in remorse he leaned upon the blade   1190
And drove it half its length into his body.
While yet the life was in him he embraced
The girl with failing arms, and breathing hard
Poured out his life-blood on to her white face.
So side by side they lie, and both are dead.
Not in this world but in the world below
He wins his bride, and shows to all mankind
That folly is the worst of human evils.

[*Exit* EURYDICE

CHORUS-LEADER. What can we think of this? The Queen is gone
    Without one word of good or evil omen.   1200

MESSENGER. What can it mean? But yet we may sustain
    The hope that she would not display her grief
    In public, but will rouse the sad lament
    For Haemon's death among her serving-women
    Inside the palace. She has true discretion,
    And she would never do what is unseemly.

CHORUS-LEADER. I cannot say, but wild lament would be
    Less ominous than this unnatural silence.

MESSENGER. It *is* unnatural; there may be danger.
    I'll follow her; it may be she is hiding   1210
    Some secret purpose in her passionate heart.

[*Exit* MESSENGER, *into the palace*

CHORUS.   Look, Creon draws near, and the burden he bears
(*anapaests*) Gives witness to his misdeeds; the cause
             Lies only in his blind error.

Enter CREON *and the* GUARDS, *with the body of* HAEMON[1]

---

[1] From this point up to the final utterance of the chorus the dialogue is in strictly
strophic form. Creon's lines, except those rendered in blank verse, are sung; they
are in the strongly-marked dochmiac rhythm.

42

Strophe 1

CREON.   Alas!
The wrongs I have done by ill-counselling!
   Cruel and fraught with death.
   You behold, men of Thebes,
The slayer, the slain; a father, a son.
My own stubborn ways have borne bitter fruit.   1220
My son! Dead, my son! So soon torn from me,
   So young, so young!
The fault only mine, not yours, O my son.

CHORUS-LEADER. Too late, too late you see the path of wisdom.

CREON.   Alas!
A bitter lesson I have learned! The god
Coming with all his weight has borne down on me,
   And smitten me with all his cruelty;
My joy overturned, trampled beneath his feet.
What suffering besets the whole race of men!   1230

Enter MESSENGER, *from the palace*

MESSENGER. My master, when you came you brought
                                                   a burden
Of sorrow with you; now, within your house,
A second store of misery confronts you.

CREON. Another sorrow come to crown my sorrow?

MESSENGER. The Queen, true mother of her son, is dead;
In grief she drove a blade into her heart.

Antistrophe 1

CREON. Alas!
Thou grim hand of death, greedy and unappeased,
   Why so implacable?
   Voice of doom, you who bring   1240
Such dire news of grief, O, can it be true?
What have you said, my son? O, you have slain the slain!

43

Tell me, can it be true? Is death crowning death?
  My wife! my wife!
My son dead, and now my wife taken too!

EURYDICE's *body is discovered*

CHORUS-LEADER. But raise your eyes: there is her lifeless body.

CREON.   Alas!
  Here is a sorrow that redoubles sorrow.
  Where will it end? What else can Fate hold in store?
  While yet I clasp my dead son in my arms   1250
  Before me there lies another struck by death.
  Alas cruel doom! the mother's and the son's.

MESSENGER. She took a sharp-edged knife, stood by the altar,
  And made lament for Megareus who was killed
  Of old, and next for Haemon. Then at last,
  Invoking evil upon you, the slayer
  Of both her sons, she closed her eyes in death.

Strophe 2

CREON. A curse, a thing of terror! O, is there none
  Will unsheathe a sword to end all my woes
  With one deadly thrust? My grief crushes me.   1260

MESSENGER. She cursed you for the guilt of Haemon's death
  And of the other son who died before.

CREON. What did she do? How did she end her life?

MESSENGER. She heard my bitter story; then she put
  A dagger to her heart and drove it home.

CREON. The guilt falls on me alone; none but I
  Have slain her; no other shares in the sin.
  'Twas I dealt the blow. This is the truth, my friends.
  Away, take me away, far from the sight of men!
  My life now is death. Lead me away from here.   1270

CHORUS-LEADER. That would be well, if anything is well.
  Briefest is best when such disaster comes.

44

Antistrophe 2

CREON. O come, best of all the days I can see,
The last day of all, the day that brings death.
O come quickly! Come, thou night with no dawn!

CHORUS-LEADER. That's for the future; here and now are duties
That fall on those to whom they are allotted.

CREON. I prayed for death; I wish for nothing else.

CHORUS-LEADER. Then pray no more; from suffering that has been
Decreed no man will ever find escape.   1280

CREON. Lead me away, a rash, a misguided man,
Whose blindness has killed a wife and a son.
O where can I look? What strength can I find?
On me has fallen a doom greater than I can bear.

                    [*Exeunt* CREON *and* GUARDS *into the palace*

CHORUS. Of happiness, far the greatest part
(anapaests) Is wisdom, and reverence towards the gods.
Proud words of the arrogant man, in the end,
Meet punishment, great as his pride was great,
Till at last he is schooled in wisdom.

OEDIPUS THE KING

DRAMATIS PERSONAE

OEDIPUS, *King of Thebes*
PRIEST OF ZEUS
CREON, *brother of Iocasta*
TEIRESIAS, *a Seer*
IOCASTA, *Queen of Thebes*
A CORINTHIAN SHEPHERD
A THEBAN SHEPHERD
A MESSENGER
Chorus of Theban citizens
Priests, Attendants, etc.

Scene: Thebes, before the royal palace

The date of the first production is unknown; probably about 425 B.C., some fifteen or twenty years after the Antigone. *The sequel,* Oedipus at Colonus, *was written much later and was first produced after Sophocles' death in 406 B.C. The three plays therefore in no real sense make a trilogy; for example, Creon appears in each, and in each is quite a different sort of man.*

The tetralogy of which the present play formed part gained the second prize; the first was awarded to an otherwise unknown Philocles, a nephew of Aeschylus. There is no need to blame the Athenian judges for not recognizing a superb play when they saw one: its fellows in the tetralogy (two more tragedies and a satyr-play) may well have been inferior.

OEDIPUS THE KING

OEDIPUS. My children, latest brood of ancient Cadmus,
What purpose brings you here, a multitude
Bearing the boughs that mark the suppliant?
Why is our air so full of frankincense,
So full of hymns and prayers and lamentations?
This, children, was no matter to entrust
To others: therefore I myself am come
Whose fame is known to all – I, Oedipus.
– You, Sir, are pointed out by length of years
To be the spokesman: tell me, what is in   10
Your hearts? What fear? What sorrow? Count on all
That I can do, for I am not so hard
As not to pity such a supplication.

PRIEST. Great King of Thebes, and sovereign Oedipus,
Look on us, who now stand before the altars –
Some young, still weak of wing; some bowed with age –
The priests, as I, of Zeus; and these, the best
Of our young men; and in the market-place,
And by Athena's temples and the shrine
Of fiery divination, there is kneeling,   20
Each with his suppliant branch, the rest of Thebes.
The city, as you see yourself, is now
Storm-tossed, and can no longer raise its head
Above the waves and angry surge of death.
The fruitful blossoms of the land are barren,
The herds upon our pastures, and our wives
In childbirth, barren. Last, and worst of all,
The withering god of fever swoops on us
To empty Cadmus' city and enrich
Dark Hades with our groans and lamentations.   30
No god we count you, that we bring our prayers,

I and these children, to your palace-door,
But wise above all other men to read
Life's riddles, and the hidden ways of Heaven;
For it was you who came and set us free
From the blood-tribute that the cruel Sphinx
Had laid upon our city; without our aid
Or our instruction, but, as we believe,
With god as ally, you gave us back our life.
So now, most dear, most mighty Oedipus,   40
We all entreat you on our bended knees,
Come to our rescue, whether from the gods
Or from some man you can find means to save.
For I have noted, *that* man's counsel is
Of best effect, who has been tried in action.
Come, noble Oedipus! Come, save our city.
Be well advised; for that past service given
This city calls you Saviour; of your kingship
Let not the record be that first we rose
From ruin, then to ruin fell again.   50
No, save our city, let it stand secure.
You brought us gladness and deliverance
Before; now do no less. You rule this land;
Better to rule it full of living men
Than rule a desert; citadel or ship
Without its company of men is nothing.

OEDIPUS. My children, what you long for, that I know
    Indeed, and pity you. I know how cruelly
    You suffer; yet, though sick, not one of you
    Suffers a sickness half as great as mine.   60
    Yours is a single pain; each man of you
    Feels but his own. My heart is heavy with
    The city's pain, my own, and yours together.
    You come to me not as to one asleep
    And needing to be wakened; many a tear
    I have been shedding, every path of thought
    Have I been pacing; and what remedy,

What single hope my anxious thought has found
That I have tried. Creon, Menoeceus' son,
My own wife's brother, I have sent to Delphi   70
To ask in Phoebus' house what act of mine,
What word of mine, may bring deliverance.
Now, as I count the days, it troubles me
What he is doing; his absence is prolonged
Beyond the proper time. But when he comes
Then write me down a villain, if I do
Not each particular that the god discloses.

PRIEST. You give us hope. – And here is more, for they
Are signalling that Creon has returned.

OEDIPUS. O Lord Apollo, even as Creon smiles,   80
Smile now on us, and let it be deliverance!

PRIEST. The news is good; or he would not be wearing
That ample wreath of richly-berried laurel.

OEDIPUS. We soon shall know; my voice will reach so far:
Creon my lord, my kinsman, what response
Do you bring with you from the god of Delphi?

Enter CREON

CREON. Good news! Our sufferings, if they are guided right,
Can even yet turn to a happy issue.

OEDIPUS. This only leaves my fear and confidence
In equal balance: what did Phoebus say?   90

CREON. Is it your wish to hear it now, in public,
Or in the palace? I am at your service.

OEDIPUS. Let them all hear! Their sufferings distress
Me more than if my own life were at stake.

CREON. Then I will tell you what Apollo said –
And it was very clear. There is pollution
Here in our midst, long-standing. This must we
Expel, nor let it grow past remedy.

51

OEDIPUS. What has defiled us? and how are we to purge it?

CREON. By banishing or killing one who murdered,   100
And so called down this pestilence upon us.

OEDIPUS. Who is the man whose death the god denounces?

CREON. Before the city passed into your care,
My lord, we had a king called Laius.

OEDIPUS. So have I often heard. – I never saw him.

CREON. His death, Apollo clearly charges us,
We must avenge upon his murderers.

OEDIPUS. Where are they now? And where shall we disclose
The unseen traces of that ancient crime?

CREON. The god said, Here. – A man who hunts with care   110
May often find what other men will miss.

OEDIPUS. Where was he murdered? In the palace here?
Or in the country? Or was he abroad?

CREON. He made a journey to consult the god,
He said – and never came back home again.

OEDIPUS. But was there no report? no fellow traveller
Whose knowledge might have helped you in your search?

CREON. All died, except one terror-stricken man,
And he could tell us nothing – next to nothing.

OEDIPUS. And what was that? One thing might lead to much, 120
If only we could find one ray of light.

CREON. He said they met with brigands – not with one,
But a whole company; they killed Laius.

OEDIPUS. A brigand would not *dare* – unless perhaps
Conspirators in Thebes had bribed the man.

CREON. There *was* conjecture; but disaster came
And we were leaderless, without our king.

OEDIPUS. Disaster? With a king cut down like that
  You did not seek the cause? Where was the hindrance?

CREON. The Sphinx. *Her* riddle pressed us harder still;   130
  For Laius – out of sight was out of mind.

OEDIPUS. I will begin again; *I'll* find the truth.
  The dead man's cause has found a true defender
  In Phoebus, and in you. And I will join you
  In seeking vengeance on behalf of Thebes
  And Phoebus too; indeed, I must: if I
  Remove this taint, it is not for a stranger,
  But for myself: the man who murdered him
  Might make the same attempt on me; and so,
  Avenging him, I shall protect myself. –   140
    Now you, my sons, without delay, arise,
  Take up your suppliant branches. – Someone, go
  And call the people here, for I will do
  What can be done; and either, by the grace
  Of God we shall be saved – or we shall fall.

PRIEST. My children, we will go; the King has promised
  All that we came to ask. – O Phoebus, thou
  Hast given us an answer: give us too
  Protection! grant remission of the plague!

            [*Exeunt* CREON, PRIESTS, *etc.* OEDIPUS *remains*

        Enter the CHORUS *representing the citizens of Thebes*

Strophe 1

CHORUS.   Sweet is the voice of the god, that
(mainly dactyls: $\frac{4}{4}$)   sounds in the   150
  Golden shrine of Delphi.
  What message has it sent to Thebes? My trembling
  Heart is torn with anguish.
  Thou god of Healing, Phoebus Apollo,
  How do I fear! What hast thou in mind
  To bring upon us now? what is to be fulfilled
  From days of old?

Tell me this, O Voice divine,
Thou child of golden Hope.

Antistrophe 1

First on the Daughter of Zeus I call for 160
Help, divine Athene;
And Artemis, whose throne is all the earth, whose
Shrine is in our city;
Apollo too, who shoots from afar:
Trinity of Powers, come to our defence!
If ever in the past, when ruin threatened us,
You stayed its course
And turned aside the flood of Death,
O then, protect us now!

Strophe 2

(agitated: $\frac{3}{8}$ *)* Past counting are the woes we suffer; 170
Affliction bears on all the city, and
Nowhere is any defence against destruction.
The holy soil can bring no increase,
Our women suffer and cry in childbirth
But do not bring forth living children.
The souls of those who perish, one by one,
Unceasingly, swift as raging fire,
Rise and take their flight to the dark realms of the dead.

Antistrophe 2

Past counting, those of us who perish:
They lie upon the ground, unpitied, 180
Unburied, infecting the air with deadly pollution.
Young wives, and grey-haired mothers with them,
From every quarter approach the altars
And cry aloud in supplication.
The prayer for healing, the loud wail of lament,
Together are heard in dissonance:
O thou golden Daughter of Zeus, grant thy aid!

Strophe 3

(mainly iambic: $\frac{3}{8}$) The fierce god of War has laid aside
His spear; but yet his terrible cry
Rings in our ears; he spreads death and destruction.   190
Ye gods, drive him back to his distant home!
  For what the light of day has spared,
  That the darkness of night destroys.
  Zeus our father! All power is thine:
The lightning-flash is thine: hurl upon him
Thy thunderbolt, and quell this god of War!

Antistrophe 3

We pray, Lord Apollo: draw thy bow
In our defence. Thy quiver is full of
Arrows unerring: shoot! slay the destroyer!
And thou, radiant Artemis, lend thy aid!   200
  Thou whose hair is bound in gold,
Bacchus, lord of the sacred dance,
  Theban Bacchus! Come, show thyself!
Display thy blazing torch; drive from our midst
The savage god, abhorred by other gods!

OEDIPUS. Would you have answer to these prayers? Then hear
My words; give heed; your help may bring
Deliverance, and the end of all our troubles.
Here do I stand before you all, a stranger
Both to the deed and to the story. – What   210
Could I have done alone, without a clue?
But I was yet a foreigner; it was later
That I became a Theban among Thebans.
So now do I proclaim to all the city:
If any Theban knows by what man's hand
He perished, Laius, son of Labdacus,
Him I command to tell me all he can;
And if he is afraid, let him annul

55

Himself the charge he fears; no punishment
Shall fall on him, save only to depart   22
Unharmed from Thebes. Further, if any knows
The slayer to be a stranger from abroad,
Let him speak out; I will reward him, and
Besides, he will have all my gratitude.
But if you still keep silent, if any man
Fearing for self or friend shall disobey me,
This will I do — and listen to my words:
Whoever he may be, I do forbid
All in this realm, of which I am the King
And high authority, to shelter in their houses   230
Or speak to him, or let him be their partner
In prayers or sacrifices to the gods, or give
Him lustral water; I command you all
To drive him from your doors; for he it is
That brings this plague upon us, as the god
Of Delphi has but now declared to me. —
So stern an ally do I make myself
Both of the god and of our murdered king. —
And for the man that slew him, whether he
Slew him alone, or with a band of helpers,   240
I lay this curse upon him, that the wretch
In wretchedness and misery may live.
And more: if with my knowledge he be found
To share my hearth and home, then upon me
Descend that doom that I invoke on him.
This charge I lay upon you, to observe
All my commands: to aid myself, the god,
And this our land, so spurned of Heaven, so ravaged.
For such a taint we should not leave unpurged —
The death of such a man, and he your king —   250
Even if Heaven had not commanded us,
But we should search it out. Now, since 'tis I
That wear the crown that he had worn before me,
And have his Queen to wife, and common children
Were born to us, but that his own did perish,

56

And sudden death has carried him away —
Because of this, I will defend his cause
As if it were my father's; nothing I
Will leave undone to find the man who killed
The son of Labdacus, and offspring of   260
Polydorus, Cadmus, and of old Agênor.
On those that disobey, this is my curse:
May never field of theirs give increase, nor
Their wives have children; may our present plagues,
And worse, be ever theirs, for their destruction.
But for the others, all with whom my words
Find favour, this I pray: Justice and all
The gods be ever at your side to help you.

CHORUS-LEADER. Your curse constrains me; therefore will I speak.
I did not kill him, neither can I tell   270
Who did. It is for Phoebus, since he laid
The task upon us, to declare the man.

OEDIPUS. True; but to force the gods against their will —
That is a thing beyond all human power.

CHORUS-LEADER. All I could say is but a second best.

OEDIPUS. Though it were third best, do not hold it back.

CHORUS-LEADER. I know of none that reads Apollo's mind
So surely as the lord Teiresias;
Consulting him you best might learn the truth.

OEDIPUS. Not even this have I neglected: Creon   280
Advised me, and already I have sent
Two messengers. – Strange he has not come.

CHORUS-LEADER. There's nothing else but old and idle gossip.

OEDIPUS. And what was that? I clutch at any straw.

CHORUS-LEADER. They said that he was killed by travellers.

OEDIPUS. So I have heard; but no one knows a witness.

CHORUS-LEADER. But if he is not proof against *all* fear
    He'll not keep silent when he hears your curse.

OEDIPUS. And will they fear a curse, who dared to kill?

CHORUS-LEADER. Here is the one to find him, for at last   290
    They bring the prophet here. He is inspired,
    The only man whose heart is filled with truth.

Enter TEIRESIAS, *led by a boy*

OEDIPUS. Teiresias, by your art you read the signs
    And secrets of the earth and of the sky;
    Therefore you know, although you cannot see,
    The plague that is besetting us; from this
    No other man but you, my lord, can save us.
    Phoebus has said – you may have heard already –
    In answer to our question, that this plague
    Will never cease unless we can discover   300
    What men they were who murdered Laius,
    And punish them with death or banishment.
    Therefore give freely all that you have learned
    From birds or other form of divination;
    Save us; save me, the city, and yourself,
    From the pollution that his bloodshed causes.
    No finer task, than to give all one has
    In helping others; we are in your hands.

TEIRESIAS. Ah! what a burden knowledge is, when knowledge
    Can be of no avail! I knew this well,   310
    And yet forgot, or I should not have come.

OEDIPUS. Why, what is this? Why are you so despondent?

TEIRESIAS. Let me go home! It will be best for you,
    And best for me, if you will let me go.

OEDIPUS. But to withhold your knowledge! This is wrong,
    Disloyal to the city of your birth.

TEIRESIAS. I know that what you say will lead you on
    To ruin; therefore, lest the same befall me too . . .

OEDIPUS. No, by the gods! Say all you know, for we
    Go down upon our knees, your suppliants.   320

TEIRESIAS. Because *you* do *not* know! I never shall
    Reveal my burden – I will not say *yours*.

OEDIPUS. You know, and will not tell us? Do you wish
    To ruin Thebes and to destroy us all?

TEIRESIAS. *My* pain, and yours, will not be caused by me.
    Why these vain questions? – for I will not speak.

OEDIPUS. You villain! – for you would provoke a stone
    To anger: you'll not speak, but show yourself
    So hard of heart and so inflexible?

TEIRESIAS. You heap the blame on me; but what is yours   330
    You do not know – therefore *I* am the villain!

OEDIPUS. And who would not be angry, finding that
    You treat our people with such cold disdain?

TEIRESIAS. The truth will come to light, without *my* help.

OEDIPUS. If it is bound to come, you ought to speak it.

TEIRESIAS. I'll say no more, and you, if so you choose,
    May rage and bluster on without restraint.

OEDIPUS. Restraint? Then I'll show none! I'll tell you all
    That I can see in you: I do believe
    This crime was planned and carried out by you,   340
    All but the killing; and were you not blind
    I'd say your hand alone had done the murder.

TEIRESIAS. So? Then I tell you this: submit yourself
    To that decree that you have made; from now
    Address no word to these men nor to me:
    You are the man whose crimes pollute our city.

OEDIPUS. What, does your impudence extend thus far?
    And do you hope that it will go scot-free?

59

TEIRESIAS. It will. I have a champion – the truth.

OEDIPUS. Who taught you that? For it was not your art.　　350

TEIRESIAS. No; you! You made me speak, against my will.

OEDIPUS. Speak what? Say it again, and say it clearly.

TEIRESIAS. Was I not clear? Or are you tempting me?

OEDIPUS. Not clear enough for me. Say it again.

TEIRESIAS. You are yourself the murderer you seek.

OEDIPUS. You'll not affront me twice and go unpunished!

TEIRESIAS. Then shall I give you still more cause for rage?

OEDIPUS. Say what you will; you'll say it to no purpose.

TEIRESIAS. *I* know, *you* do not know, the hideous life
Of shame you lead with those most near to you.　　360

OEDIPUS. You'll pay most dearly for this insolence!

TEIRESIAS. No, not if Truth is strong, and can prevail.

OEDIPUS. It is – except in you; for you are blind
In eyes and ears and brains and everything.

TEIRESIAS. You'll not forget these insults that you throw
At me, when all men throw the same at you.

ODEIPUS. You live in darkness; you can do no harm
To me or any man who has his eyes.

TEIRESIAS. No; *I* am not to bring you down, because
Apollo is enough; he'll see to it.　　370

OEDIPUS. Creon, or you? Which of you made this plot?

TEIRESIAS. Creon's no enemy of yours; you are your own.

OEDIPUS. O Wealth! O Royalty! whose commanding art
Outstrips all other arts in life's contentions!
How great a store of envy lies upon you,
If for this sceptre, that the city gave

Freely to me, unasked – if now my friend,
The trusty Creon, burns to drive me hence
And steal it from me! So he has suborned
This crafty schemer here, this mountebank,   380
Whose purse alone has eyes, whose art is blind. –
Come, prophet, show your title! When the Sphinx
Chanted her music here, why did not *you*
Speak out and save the city? Yet such a question
Was one for augury, not for mother wit.
You were no prophet then; your birds, your voice
From Heaven, were dumb. But I, who came by chance,
I, knowing nothing, put the Sphinx to flight,
Thanks to my wit – no thanks to divination!
And now you try to drive me out; you hope   390
When Creon's king to bask in Creon's favour.
You'll expiate the curse? Ay, and repent it,
Both you and your accomplice. But that you
Seem old, I'd teach you what you gain by treason!

CHORUS-LEADER. My lord, he spoke in anger; so, I think,
    Did you. What help in angry speeches? Come,
    This is the task, how we can best discharge
    The duty that the god has laid on us.

TEIRESIAS. King though you are, I claim the privilege
    Of equal answer. No, I have the right;   400
    I am no slave of yours – I serve Apollo,
    And therefore am not listed *Creon's* man.
    Listen – since you have taunted me with blindness!
    You have your sight, and yet you cannot see
    Where, nor with whom, you live, nor in what horror.
    Your parents – do you know them? or that you
    Are enemy to your kin, alive or dead?
    And that a father's and a mother's curse
    Shall join to drive you headlong out of Thebes
    And change the light that now you see to darkness?   410
    Your cries of agony, where will they not reach?
    Where on Cithaeron will they not re-echo?

61

When you have learned what meant the marriage-song
Which bore you to an evil haven here
After so fair a voyage? And you are blind
To other horrors, which shall make you one
With your own children. Therefore, heap your scorn
On Creon and on me, for no man living
Will meet a doom more terrible than yours.

OEDIPUS. What? Am I to suffer words like this from him?   420
Ruin, damnation seize you! Off at once
Out of our sight! Go! Get you whence you came!

TEIRESIAS. Had you not called me, I should not be here.

OEDIPUS. And had I known that you would talk such folly,
I'd not have called you to a house of mine.

TEIRESIAS. To you I seem a fool, but to your parents,
To those who did beget you, I was wise.

OEDIPUS. Stop! Who were they? Who *were* my parents? Tell me!

TEIRESIAS. This day will show your birth and your destruction.

OEDIPUS. You are too fond of dark obscurities.   430

TEIRESIAS. But do you not excel in reading riddles?

OEDIPUS. I scorn your taunts; my skill has brought me glory.

TEIRESIAS. And this success brought you to ruin too.

OEDIPUS. I am content, if so I saved this city.

TEIRESIAS. Then I will leave you. Come, boy, take my hand.

OEDIPUS. Yes, let him take it. You are nothing but
Vexation here. Begone, and give me peace!

TEIRESIAS. When I have had my say. No frown of yours
Shall frighten *me*; you cannot injure me.
Here is my message: that man whom you seek   440
With threats and proclamations for the death
Of Laius, he is living here; he's thought
To be a foreigner, but shall be found
Theban by birth – and little joy will this

62

Bring *him*; when, with his eyesight turned to blindness,
His wealth to beggary, on foreign soil
With staff in hand he'll tap his way along,
His children with him; and he will be known
Himself to be their father and their brother,
The husband of the mother who gave him birth,　　　　450
Supplanter of his father, and his slayer.
– There! Go, and think on this; and if you find
That I'm deceived, say then – and not before –
That I am ignorant in divination.

　　　　　　　[*Exeunt severally* TEIRESIAS *and* OEDIPUS

Strophe 1

CHORUS. The voice of god rang out in the holy cavern,
　　Denouncing one who has killed a King – the crime of crimes.
　　　　Who is the man? Let him begone in
　　　　Headlong flight, swift as a horse!

(*anapaests*) For the terrible god, like a warrior armed,
　　Stands ready to strike with a lightning-flash:　　　460
　　　　The Furies who punish crime, and never fail,
　　　　Are hot in their pursuit.

Antistrophe 1

The snow is white on the cliffs of high Parnassus.
It has flashed a message: Let every Theban join the hunt!
　　　Lurking in caves among the mountains,
　　　Deep in the woods – where is the man?

(*anapaests*) In wearisome flight, unresting, alone,
　　An outlaw, he shuns Apollo's shrine;
　　　　But ever the living menace of the god
　　　　Hovers around his head.　　　　470

Strophe 2

(*choriambics*) Strange, disturbing, what the wise
　　Prophet has said. What can he mean?

Neither can I believe, nor can I disbelieve;
I do not know what to say.
I look here, and there; nothing can I find –
No strife, either now or in the past,
Between the kings of Thebes and Corinth.
A hand unknown struck down the King;
Though I would learn who it was dealt the blow,
That *he* is guilty whom all revere –   480
How can I believe this with no proof?

Antistrophe 2

Zeus, Apollo – they have knowledge;
They understand the ways of life.
Prophets are men, like me; that they can understand
More than is revealed to me –
Of that, I can find nowhere certain proof,
Though one man is wise, another foolish.
Until the charge is manifest
I will not credit his accusers.
I saw myself how the Sphinx challenged him: 490
He proved his wisdom; he saved our city;
Therefore how can I now condemn him?

Enter CREON

CREON. They tell me, Sirs, that Oedipus the King
Has made against me such an accusation
That I will not endure. For if he thinks
That in this present trouble I have done
Or said a single thing to do him harm,
Then let me die, and not drag out my days
With such a name as that. For it is not
One injury this accusation does me;   500
It touches my whole life, if you, my friends,
And all the city are to call me traitor.

CHORUS-LEADER. The accusation may perhaps have come
From heat of temper, not from sober judgement.

CREON. What was it made him think contrivances
    Of mine suborned the seer to tell his lies?

CHORUS-LEADER. Those were his words; I do not know his
                                                        reasons.

CREON. Was he in earnest, master of himself,
    When he attacked me with this accusation?

CHORUS-LEADER. I do not closely scan what kings are
                                                doing. – 510
    But here he comes in person from the palace.

Enter OEDIPUS

OEDIPUS. What, *you*? You dare come here? How can you find
    The impudence to show yourself before
    My house, when you are clearly proven
    To have sought my life and tried to steal my crown?
    Why, do you think me then a coward, or
    A fool, that you should try to lay this plot?
    Or that I should not see what you were scheming,
    And so fall unresisting, blindly, to you?
    But you were mad, so to attempt the throne,   520
    Poor and unaided; this is not encompassed
    Without the strong support of friends and money!

CREON. This you must do: now you have had your say
    Hear my reply; then yourself shall judge.

OEDIPUS. A ready tongue! But I am bad at listening –
    To you. For I have found how much you hate me.

CREON. One thing: first listen to what I have to say.

OEDIPUS. One thing: do not pretend you're not a villain.

CREON. If you believe it is a thing worth having,
    Insensate stubbornness, then you are wrong.   530

OEDIPUS. If you believe that one can harm a kinsman
    Without retaliation, you are wrong.

65

CREON. With this I have no quarrel; but explain
What injury you say that I have done you.

OEDIPUS. Did you advise, or did you not, that I
Should send a man for that most reverend prophet?

CREON. I did, and I am still of that advice.

OEDIPUS. How long a time is it since Laius . . .

CREON. Since Laius did *what?* How can I say?

OEDIPUS. Was seen no more, but met a violent death?   540

CREON. It would be many years now past and gone.

OEDIPUS. And had this prophet learned his art already?

CREON. Yes; his repute was great – as it is now.

OEDIPUS. Did he make any mention then of me?

CREON. He never spoke of you within my hearing.

OEDIPUS. Touching the murder: did you make no search?

CREON. No search? Of course we did; but we found nothing.

OEDIPUS. And why did this wise prophet not speak *then?*

CREON. Who knows? Where I know nothing I say nothing.

OEDIPUS. This much you know – and you'll do well to
answer: 550

CREON. What is it? If I know, I'll tell you freely.

OEDIPUS. That if he had not joined with you, he'd not
Have said that I was Laius' murderer.

CREON. If he said this, I did not know. – But I
May rightly question you, as you have me.

OEDIPUS. Ask what you will. You'll never prove *I* killed him.

CREON. Why then: are you not married to my sister?

OEDIPUS. I am indeed; it cannot be denied.

66

CREON. You share with her the sovereignty of Thebes?

OEDIPUS. She need but ask, and anything is hers. 560

CREON. And am I not myself conjoined with you?

OEDIPUS. You are; not rebel therefore, but a traitor!

CREON. Not so, if you will reason with yourself,
As I with you. This first: would any man,
To gain no increase of authority,
Choose kingship, with its fears and sleepless nights?
Not I. What I desire, what every man
Desires, if he has wisdom, is to take
The substance, not the show, of royalty.
For now, through you, I have both power and ease, 570
But were I king, I'd be oppressed with cares.
Not so: while I have ample sovereignty
And rule in peace, why should I want the crown?
I am not yet so mad as to give up
All that which brings me honour and advantage.
Now, every man greets me, and I greet him;
Those who have need of you make much of me,
Since I can make or mar them. Why should I
Surrender this to load myself with that?
A man of sense was never yet a traitor; 580
I have no taste for that, nor could I force
Myself to aid another's treachery.
    But you can test me: go to Delphi; ask
If I reported rightly what was said.
And further: if you find that I had dealings
With that diviner, you may take and kill me
Not with your single vote, but yours and mine,
But not on bare suspicion, unsupported.
How wrong it is, to use a random judgement
And think the false man true, the true man false! 590
To spurn a loyal friend, that is no better
Than to destroy the life to which we cling.
This you will learn in time, for Time alone

67

Reveals the upright man; a single day
Suffices to unmask the treacherous.

CHORUS-LEADER. My lord, he speaks with caution, to avoid
Grave error. Hasty judgement is not sure.

OEDIPUS. But when an enemy is quick to plot
And strike, I must be quick in answer too.
If I am slow, and wait, then I shall find   600
That he has gained his end, and I am lost.

CREON. What do you wish? To drive me into exile?

OEDIPUS. No, more than exile: I will have your life.[1]

CREON. ⟨When will it cease, this monstrous rage of yours?⟩

OEDIPUS. When your example shows what comes of envy.

CREON. Must you be stubborn? Cannot you believe me?

OEDIPUS. ⟨You speak to me as if I were a fool!⟩

CREON. Because I know you're wrong.

OEDIPUS   Right, for myself!

CREON. It is not right for me!

OEDIPUS.   But you're a traitor.

CREON. What if your charge is false?

OEDIPUS.   I have to govern.   610

----

[1] The next two verses, as they stand in the MSS., are impossible. Editors are
agreed on this, though no single remedy has found general acceptance. The MSS.
attribute v. 624 (v. 605 here) to Creon, and v. 625 (v. 606 here) to Oedipus. I
can make no real sense of this: the only φθόνος, 'envy', that is in question is the
envy of his royal power that Oedipus is attributing to Creon; and the words
ὑπείξων, 'yield', 'not to be stubborn', and πιστεύσων, 'believe', must surely be
used by Creon of Oedipus, not by Oedipus of Creon. Since a translator who hopes
to be acted must give the actors something to say, preferably good sense, and
cannot fob them off with a row of dots, I have reconstructed the passage by guess-
work, putting my guesses within brackets. I have assumed that two verses were
lost, one after v. 623 and one after v. 625, and that the wrong attribution of
vv. 624 and 625 followed almost inevitably.

CREON. Not govern badly!

OEDIPUS.   Listen to him, Thebes!

CREON. You're not the city! I am Theban too.

CHORUS-LEADER. My lords, no more! Here comes the Queen,
                                                    and not
Too soon, to join you. With her help, you must
Compose the bitter strife that now divides you.

Enter IOCASTA

IOCASTA. You frantic men! What has aroused this wild
Dispute? Have you no shame, when such a plague
Afflicts us, to indulge in private quarrels?
Creon, go home, I pray. You, Oedipus,
Come in; do not make much of what is nothing.

CREON. My sister: Oedipus, your husband here,   620
Has thought it right to punish me with one
Of two most awful dooms: exile, or death.

OEDIPUS. I have: I have convicted him, Iocasta,
Of plotting secretly against my life.

CREON. If I am guilty in a single point
Of such a crime, then may I die accursed.

IOCASTA. O, by the gods, believe him, Oedipus!
Respect the oath that he has sworn, and have
Regard for me, and for these citizens.

*(In what follows, the parts given to the chorus are sung, the rest,
presumably, spoken. The rhythm of the music and dance is either
dochmiac, 5-time, or a combination of 3- and 5-time.)*

Strophe

CHORUS. My lord, I pray, give consent.   630
Yield to us; ponder well.

OEDIPUS. What is it you would have me yield?

CHORUS. Respect a man ripe in years,
  Bound by this mighty oath he has sworn.

OEDIPUS. Your wish is clear?

CHORUS.   It is.

OEDIPUS.   Then tell it me.

CHORUS. Not to repel, and drive out of our midst a friend,
  Scorning a solemn curse, for uncertain cause.

OEDIPUS. I tell you this: your prayer will mean for me
  My banishment from Thebes, or else my death.

CHORUS. No, no! by the Sun, the chief of gods,   640
    Ruin and desolation and all evil come upon me
  If I harbour thoughts such as these!
  No; our land racked with plague breaks my heart.
    Do not now deal a new wound on Thebes to crown the old!

OEDIPUS. Then let him be, though I must die twice over,
  Or be dishonoured, spurned and driven out.
  It's your entreaty, and not his, that moves
  My pity; he shall have my lasting hatred.

CREON. You yield ungenerously; but when your wrath
  Has cooled, how it will prick you! Natures such   650
  As yours give most vexation to themselves.

OEDIPUS. O, let me be! Get from my sight.

CREON.   I go,
  Misjudged by you – but these will judge me better [*indicating*
                                          CHORUS].
                                          [*Exit* CREON

Antistrophe

CHORUS. My lady, why now delay?
  Let the King go in with you.

IOCASTA. When you have told me what has passed.

70

CHORUS. Suspicion came. – Random words, undeserved,
Will provoke men to wrath.

IOCASTA. It was from both?

CHORUS.   It was.

IOCASTA.   And what was said?

CHORUS. It is enough for me, more than enough, when I   660
Think of our ills, that this should rest where it lies.

OEDIPUS. You and your wise advice, blunting my wrath,
Frustrated me – and it has come to this!

CHORUS. This, O my King, I said, and say again:
I should be mad, distraught,
I should be a fool, and worse,
If I sought to drive you away.
Thebes was near sinking; you brought her safe
Through the storm. Now again we pray that you may save us.

IOCASTA. In Heaven's name, my lord, I too must know   670
What was the reason for this blazing anger.

OEDIPUS. There's none to whom I more defer; and so,
I'll tell you: Creon and his vile plot against me.

IOCASTA. What has he done, that you are so incensed?

OEDIPUS. He says that I am Laius' murderer.

IOCASTA. From his own knowledge? Or has someone told him?

OEDIPUS. No; that suspicion should not fall upon
Himself, he used a tool – a crafty prophet.

IOCASTA. Why, have no fear of *that*. Listen to me,
And you will learn that the prophetic art   680
Touches our human fortunes not at all.
I soon can give you proof. – An oracle
Once came to Laius – from the god himself
I do not say, but from his ministers:
His fate it was, that should he have a son
By me, that son would take his father's life.

71

But he was killed – or so they said – by strangers,
By brigands, at a place where three ways meet.
As for the child, it was not three days old
When Laius fastened both its feet together   690
And had it cast over a precipice.
Therefore Apollo failed; for neither did
His son kill Laius, nor did Laius meet
The awful end he feared, killed by his son.
     So much for what prophetic voices uttered.
Have no regard for them. The god will bring
To light himself whatever thing he chooses.

OEDIPUS. Iocasta, terror seizes me, and shakes
     My very soul, at one thing you have said.

IOCASTA. Why so? What have I said to frighten you?   700

OEDIPUS. I think I heard you say that Laius
     Was murdered at a place where three ways meet?

IOCASTA. So it was said – indeed, they say it still.

OEDIPUS. Where is the place where this encounter happened?

IOCASTA. They call the country Phokis, and a road
     From Delphi joins a road from Daulia.

OEDIPUS. Since that was done, how many years have passed?

IOCASTA. It was proclaimed in Thebes a little time
     Before the city offered you the crown.

OEDIPUS. O Zeus, what fate hast thou ordained for me?   710

IOCASTA. What is the fear that so oppresses you?

OEDIPUS. One moment yet: tell me of Laius.
     What age was he? and what was his appearance?

IOCASTA. A tall man, and his hair was touched with white;
     In figure he was not unlike yourself.

OEDIPUS. O God! Did I, then, in my ignorance,
     Proclaim that awful curse against myself?

IOCASTA. What are you saying? How you frighten me!

OEDIPUS. I greatly fear that prophet was not blind.
But yet one question; that will show me more.   720

IOCASTA. For all my fear, I'll tell you what I can.

OEDIPUS. Was he alone, or did he have with him
A royal bodyguard of men-at-arms?

IOCASTA. The company in all were five; the King
Rode in a carriage, and there was a Herald.

OEDIPUS. Ah God! How clear the picture is! . . . But who,
Iocasta, brought report of this to Thebes?

IOCASTA. A slave, the only man that was not killed.

OEDIPUS. And is he round about the palace now?

IOCASTA. No, he is not. When he returned, and saw   730
You ruling in the place of the dead King,
He begged me, on his bended knees, to send him
Into the hills as shepherd, out of sight,
As far as could be from the city here.
I sent him, for he was a loyal slave;
He well deserved this favour – and much more.

OEDIPUS. Could he be brought back here – at once – to see me?

IOCASTA. He could; but why do you desire his coming?

OEDIPUS. I fear I have already said, Iocasta,
More than enough; and therefore I will see him.   740

IOCASTA. Then he shall come. But, as your wife, I ask you,
What is the terror that possesses you?

OEDIPUS. And you shall know it, since my fears have grown
So great; for who is more to me than you,
That I should speak to *him* at such a moment?
    My father, then, was Polybus of Corinth;
My mother, Merope. My station there
Was high as any man's – until a thing
Befell me that was strange indeed, though not

73

Deserving of the thought I gave to it.   750
A man said at a banquet – he was full
Of wine – that I was not my father's son.
It angered me; but I restrained myself
That day. The next I went and questioned both
My parents. They were much incensed with him
Who had let fall the insult. So, from them,
I had assurance. Yet the slander spread
And always chafed me. Therefore secretly,
My mother and my father unaware,
I went to Delphi. Phoebus would return   760
No answer to my question, but declared
A thing most horrible: he foretold that I
Should mate with my own mother, and beget
A brood that men would shudder to behold,
And that I was to be the murderer
Of my own father.
                    Therefore, back to Corinth
I never went – the stars alone have told me
Where Corinth lies – that I might never see
Cruel fulfilment of that oracle.
So journeying, I came to that same spot   770
Where, as you say, this King was killed. And now,
This is the truth, Iocasta: when I reached
The place where three ways meet, I met a herald,
And in a carriage drawn by colts was such
A man as you describe. By violence
The herald and the older man attempted
To push me off the road, I, in my rage,
Struck at the driver, who was hustling me.
The old man, when he saw me level with him,
Taking a double-goad, aimed at my head   780
A murderous blow. He paid for that, full measure.
Swiftly I hit him with my staff; he rolled
Out of his carriage, flat upon his back.
I killed them all. – But if, between this stranger
And Laius there was any bond of kinship,

74

Who could be in more desperate plight than I?
Who more accursèd in the eyes of Heaven?
For neither citizen nor stranger may
Receive me in his house, nor speak to me,
But he must bar the door. And it was none   790
But I invoked this curse on my own head!
And I pollute the bed of him I slew
With my own hands! Say, am I vile? Am I
Not all impure? Seeing I must be exiled,
And even in my exile must not go
And see my parents, nor set foot upon
My native land; or, if I do, I must
Marry my mother, and kill Polybus
My father, who engendered me and reared me.
If one should say it was a cruel god   800
Brought this upon me, would he not speak right?
    No, no, you holy powers above! Let me
Not see that day! but rather let me pass
Beyond the sight of men, before I see
The stain of such pollution come upon me!

CHORUS-LEADER. My lord, this frightens me. But you must hope,
    Until we hear the tale from him that saw it.

OEDIPUS. That is the only hope that's left to me;
    We must await the coming of the shepherd.

IOCASTA. What do you hope from him, when he is here?   810

OEDIPUS. I'll tell you: if his story shall be found
    The same as yours, then I am free of guilt.

IOCASTA. But what have *I* said of especial note?

OEDIPUS. You said that he reported it was brigands
    Who killed the King. If he still speaks of 'men',
    It was not I; a single man, and 'men',
    Are not the same. But if he says it was
    A traveller journeying alone, why then,
    The burden of the guilt must fall on me.

IOCASTA. But that *is* what he said, I do assure you!　　820
　　He cannot take it back again! Not I
　　Alone, but the whole city heard him say it!
　　But even if he should revoke the tale
　　He told before, not even so, my lord,
　　Will he establish that the King was slain
　　According to the prophecy. For that was clear:
　　His son, and mine, should slay him. – He, poor thing,
　　Was killed himself, and never killed his father.
　　Therefore, so far as divination goes,
　　Or prophecy, I'll take no notice of it.　　830

OEDIPUS. And that is wise. – But send a man to bring
　　The shepherd; I would not have that neglected.

IOCASTA. I'll send at once. – But come with me; for I
　　Would not do anything that could displease you.

　　　　　　　　　　[*Exeunt* OEDIPUS *and* IOCASTA

Strophe 1

CHORUS. I pray that I may pass my life
(in a steady rhythm) In reverent holiness of word and deed.
　　For there are laws enthroned above;
　　Heaven created them,
　　Olympus was their father,
　　And mortal men had no part in their birth;　　840
　　Nor ever shall their power pass from sight
　　In dull forgetfulness;
　　A god moves in them; he grows not old.

Antistrophe 1

Pride makes the tyrant – pride of wealth
And power, too great for wisdom and restraint;
For Pride will climb the topmost height;
Then is the man cast down
To uttermost destruction.
There he finds no escape, no resource.
But high contention for the city's good　　850

76

May the gods preserve.
For me – may the gods be my defence!

Strophe 2

If there is one who walks in pride
Of word or deed, and has no fear of Justice,
No reverence for holy shrines –
May utter ruin fall on him!
So may his ill-starred pride be given its reward.
Those who seek dishonourable advantage
And lay violent hands on holy things
And do not shun impiety –   860
Who among these will secure himself from the wrath of God?
If deeds like these are honoured,
Why should I join in the sacred dance?

Antistrophe 2

No longer shall Apollo's shrine,
The holy centre of the Earth, receive my worship;
No, nor his seat at Abae, nor
The temple of Olympian Zeus,
If what the god foretold does not come to pass.
Mighty Zeus – if so I should address Thee –
O great Ruler of all things, look on this!   870
Now are thy oracles falling into contempt, and men
Deny Apollo's power.
Worship of the gods is passing away.

Enter IOCASTA, *attended by a girl carrying a wreath and incense*

IOCASTA. My lords of Thebes, I have bethought myself
   To approach the altars of the gods, and lay
   These wreaths on them, and burn this frankincense.
   For every kind of terror has laid hold
   On Oedipus; his judgement is distracted.
   He will not read the future by the past
   But yields himself to any who speaks fear.   880

77

Since then no words of mine suffice to calm him
I turn to Thee, Apollo – Thou art nearest –
Thy suppliant, with these votive offerings.
Grant us deliverance and peace, for now
Fear is on all, when we see Oedipus,
The helmsman of the ship, so terrified.

(*A reverent silence, while* IOCASTA *lays the wreath at the altar and sets fire to the incense. The wreath will remain and the incense smoke during the rest of the play.*)

Enter a SHEPHERD FROM CORINTH

CORINTHIAN. Might I inquire of you where I may find
　The royal palace of King Oedipus?
　Or, better, where himself is to be found?

CHORUS-LEADER. There is the palace; himself, Sir, is within,　890
　But here his wife and mother of his children.

CORINTHIAN. Ever may happiness attend on her,
　And hers, the wedded wife of such a man.

IOCASTA. May you enjoy the same; your gentle words
　Deserve no less. – Now, Sir, declare your purpose;
　With what request, what message have you come?

CORINTHIAN. With good news for your husband and his house.

IOCASTA. What news is this? And who has sent you here?

CORINTHIAN. I come from Corinth, and the news I bring
　Will give you joy, though joy be crossed with grief.　900

IOCASTA. What is this, with its two-fold influence?

CORINTHIAN. The common talk in Corinth is that they
　Will call on Oedipus to be their king.

IOCASTA. What? Does old Polybus no longer reign?

CORINTHIAN. Not now, for Death has laid him in his grave.

IOCASTA. Go quickly to your master, girl; give him
　The news. – You oracles, where are you now?
　This is the man whom Oedipus so long

78

Has shunned, fearing to kill him; now he's dead,
And killed by Fortune, not by Oedipus.   910

Enter OEDIPUS, *very nervous*

OEDIPUS. My dear Iocasta, tell me, my dear wife,
Why have you sent to fetch me from the palace?

IOCASTA. Listen to *him,* and as you hear, reflect
What has become of all those oracles.

OEDIPUS. Who is this man? – What has he to tell me?

IOCASTA. He is from Corinth, and he brings you news
About your father. Polybus is dead.

OEDIPUS. What say you, sir? Tell me the news yourself.

CORINTHIAN. If you would have me first report on this,
I tell you; death has carried him away.   920

OEDIPUS. By treachery? Or did sickness come to him?

CORINTHIAN. A small mischance will lay an old man low.

OEDIPUS. Poor Polybus! He died, then, of a sickness?

CORINTHIAN. That, and the measure of his many years.

OEDIPUS. Ah me! Why then, Iocasta, should a man
Regard the Pythian house of oracles,
Or screaming birds, on whose authority
I was to slay my father? But he is dead;
The earth has covered him; and here am I,
My sword undrawn – unless perchance *my* loss   930
Has killed him; so might I be called his slayer.
But for those oracles about my father,
Those he has taken with him to the grave
Wherein he lies, and they are come to nothing.

IOCASTA. Did I not say long since it would be so?

OEDIPUS. You did; but I was led astray by fear.

IOCASTA. So none of this deserves another thought.

OEDIPUS. Yet how can I not fear my mother's bed?

79

IOCASTA. Why should we fear, seeing that man is ruled
   By chance, and there is room for no clear forethought?   940
   No; live at random, live as best one can.
   So do not fear this marriage with your mother;
   Many a man has suffered this before –
   But only in his dreams. Whoever thinks
   The least of this, he lives most comfortably.

OEDIPUS. Your every word I do accept, if she
   That bore me did not live; but as she does –
   Despite your wisdom, how can I but tremble?

IOCASTA. Yet there is comfort in your father's death.

OEDIPUS. Great comfort, but still fear of her who lives.   950

CORINTHIAN. And who is this who makes you so afraid?

OEDIPUS. Meropê, my man, the wife of Polybus.

CORINTHIAN. And what in *her* gives cause of fear in *you*?

OEDIPUS. There was an awful warning from the gods.

CORINTHIAN. Can it be told, or must it be kept secret?

OEDIPUS. No secret. Once Apollo said that I
   Was doomed to lie with my own mother, and
   Defile my own hands with my father's blood.
   Wherefore has Corinth been, these many years,
   My home no more. My fortunes have been fair. –   960
   But it is good to see a parent's face.

CORINTHIAN. It was for fear of *this* you fled the city?

OEDIPUS. This, and the shedding of my father's blood.

CORINTHIAN. Why then, my lord, since I am come in friendship,
   I'll rid you here and now of that misgiving.

OEDIPUS. Be sure, your recompense would be in keeping.

CORINTHIAN. It was the chief cause of my coming here
   That your return might bring me some advantage.

OEDIPUS. Back to my parents I will never go.

CORINTHIAN. My son, it is clear, you know not what you
do. 970

OEDIPUS. Not know? What is this? Tell me what you mean.

CORINTHIAN. If for this reason you avoid your home.

OEDIPUS. Fearing Apollo's oracle may come true.

CORINTHIAN. And you incur pollution from your parents?

OEDIPUS. That is the thought that makes me live in terror.

CORINTHIAN. I tell you then, this fear of yours is idle.

OEDIPUS. How? Am I not their child, and they my parents?

CORINTHIAN. Because there's none of Polybus in you.

OEDIPUS. How can you say so? Was he not my father?

CORINTHIAN. I am your father just as much as he! 980

OEDIPUS. A stranger equal to the father? How?

CORINTHIAN. Neither did he beget you, nor did I.

OEDIPUS. Then for what reason did he call me son?

CORINTHIAN. He had you as a gift – from my own hands.

OEDIPUS. And showed such love to me? Me, not his own?

CORINTHIAN. Yes; his own childlessness so worked on him.

OEDIPUS. You, when you gave me: had you bought, or found me?

CORINTHIAN. I found you in the woods upon Cithaeron.

OEDIPUS. Why were you travelling in that neighbourhood?

CORINTHIAN. I tended flocks of sheep upon the mountain. 990

OEDIPUS. You were a shepherd, then, wandering for hire?

CORINTHIAN. I was, my son; but that day, your preserver.

81

OEDIPUS. How so? What ailed me when you took me up?

CORINTHIAN. For that, your ankles might give evidence.

OEDIPUS. Alas! why speak of this, my life-long trouble?

CORINTHIAN. I loosed the fetters clamped upon your feet.

OEDIPUS. A pretty gift to carry from the cradle!

CORINTHIAN. It was for this they named you Oedipus.

OEDIPUS. Who did, my father or my mother? Tell me.

CORINTHIAN. I cannot; he knows more, from whom I had
you.   1000

OEDIPUS. It was another, not yourself, that found me?

CORINTHIAN. Yes, you were given me by another shepherd.

OEDIPUS. Who? Do you know him? Can you name the man?

CORINTHIAN. They said that he belonged to Laius.

OEDIPUS. What – him who once was ruler here in Thebes?

CORINTHIAN. Yes, he it was for whom this man was shepherd.

OEDIPUS. And is he still alive, that I can see him?

CORINTHIAN [*turning to the Chorus*].
  You that are native here would know that best.

OEDIPUS. Has any man of you now present here
  Acquaintance with this shepherd, him he speaks of?   1010
  Has any seen him, here, or in the fields?
  Speak; on this moment hangs discovery.

CHORUS-LEADER. It is, I think, the man that you have sent for,
  The slave now in the country. But who should know
  The truth of this more than Iocasta here?

OEDIPUS. The man he speaks of: do you think, Iocasta,
  He is the one I have already summoned?

IOCASTA. What matters who he is? Pay no regard. –
  The tale is idle; it is best forgotten.   1020

82

OEDIPUS. It cannot be that I should have this clue
 And then not find the secret of my birth.

IOCASTA. In God's name stop, if you have any thought
 For your own life! My ruin is enough.

OEDIPUS. Be not dismayed; nothing can prove you base.
 Not though I find my mother thrice a slave.

IOCASTA. O, I beseech you, do not! Seek no more!

OEDIPUS. You cannot move me. I *will* know the truth.

IOCASTA. I know that what I say is for the best.

OEDIPUS. This 'best' of yours! I have no patience with it.

IOCASTA. O may you never learn what man you are!   1030

OEDIPUS. Go, someone, bring the herdsman here to me,
 And leave her to enjoy her pride of birth.

IOCASTA. O man of doom! For by no other name
 Can I address you now or evermore.

                                        [*Exit* IOCASTA

CHORUS-LEADER. The Queen has fled, my lord, as if before
 Some driving storm of grief. I fear that from
 Her silence may break forth some great disaster.

OEDIPUS. Break forth what will! My birth, however humble,
 I am resolved to find. But she, perhaps,
 Is proud, as women will be; is ashamed   1040
 Of my low birth. But I do rate myself
 The child of Fortune, giver of all good,
 And I shall not be put to shame, for I
 Am born of Her; the Years who are my kinsmen
 Distinguished my estate, now high, now low;
 So born, I could not make me someone else,
 And not do all to find my parentage.

Strophe 1

CHORUS. If I have power of prophecy,
(animated rhythm) If I have judgement wise and sure, Cithaeron
                            83

(I swear by Olympus),
Thou shalt be honoured when the moon
Next is full, as mother and foster-nurse
And birth-place of Oedipus, with festival and dancing,
For thou hast given great blessings to our King.
To Thee, Apollo, now we raise our cry:
O grant our prayer find favour in thy sight!

Antistrophe

Who is thy mother, O my son?
Is she an ageless nymph among the mountains,
That bore thee to Pan?
Or did Apollo father thee?   1060
For dear to him are the pastures in the hills.
Or Hermes, who ruleth from the summit of Kyllene?
Or Dionysus on the mountain-tops,
Did he receive thee from thy mother's arms,
A nymph who follows him on Helicon?

OEDIPUS. If I, who never yet have met the man,
  May risk conjecture, I think I see the herdsman
  Whom we have long been seeking. In his age
  He well accords; and more, I recognize
  Those who are with him as of my own household.   1070
  But as for knowing, you will have advantage
  Of me, if you have seen the man before.

CHORUS-LEADER. 'Tis he, for certain – one of Laius' men,
  One of the shepherds whom he trusted most.

Enter the THEBAN SHEPHERD

OEDIPUS. You first I ask, you who have come from Corinth:
  Is that the man you mean?

CORINTHIAN.   That very man.

OEDIPUS. Come here, my man; look at me; answer me
  My questions. Were you ever Laius' man?

THEBAN. I was; his slave – born in the house, not bought.

OEDIPUS. What was your charge, or what your way of life?　1080

THEBAN. Tending the sheep, the most part of my life.

OEDIPUS. And to what regions did you most resort?

THEBAN. Now it was Cithaeron, now the country round.

OEDIPUS. And was this man of your acquaintance there?

THEBAN. In what employment? Which is the man you mean?

OEDIPUS. Him yonder. Had you any dealings with him?

THEBAN. Not such that I can quickly call to mind.

CORINTHIAN. No wonder, Sir, but though he has forgotten
I can remind him. I am very sure,
He knows the time when, round about Cithaeron,　1090
He with a double flock, and I with one,
We spent together three whole summer seasons,
From spring until the rising of Arcturus.
Then, with the coming on of winter, I
Drove my flocks home, he his, to Laius' folds.
Is this the truth? or am I telling lies?

THEBAN. It is true, although it happened long ago.

CORINTHIAN. Then tell me: do you recollect a baby
You gave me once to bring up for my own?

THEBAN. Why this? Why are you asking me this question?

CORINTHIAN. My friend, *here* is the man who was that baby!　1100

THEBAN. O, devil take you! Cannot you keep silent?

OEDIPUS. Here, Sir! This man needs no reproof from you.
Your tongue needs chastisement much more than his.

THEBAN. O best of masters, how am I offending?

OEDIPUS. Not telling of the child of whom he speaks.

THEBAN. He? He knows nothing. He is wasting time.

OEDIPUS [*threatening*]. If you'll not speak from pleasure, speak
from pain.

THEBAN. No, no, I pray! Not torture an old man!

OEDIPUS. Here, someone, quickly! Twist this fellow's arms!

THEBAN. Why, wretched man? What would you know
besides?   1110

OEDIPUS. That child: you gave it him, the one he speaks of?

THEBAN. I did. Ah God, would I had died instead!

OEDIPUS. And die you shall, unless you speak the truth.

THEBAN. And if I do, then death is still more certain.

OEDIPUS. This man, I think, is trying to delay me.

THEBAN. Not I! I said I gave the child – just now.

OEDIPUS. And got it – where? Your own? or someone else's?

THEBAN. No, not my own. Someone had given it me.

OEDIPUS. Who? Which of these our citizens? From what house?

THEBAN. No, I implore you, master! Do not ask!   1120

OEDIPUS. You die if I must question you again.

THEBAN. Then, 'twas a child of one in Laius' house.

OEDIPUS. You mean a slave? Or someone of his kin?

THEBAN. God! I am on the verge of saying it.

OEDIPUS. And I of hearing it, but hear I must.

THEBAN. His own, or so they said. But she within
Could tell you best – your wife – the truth of it.

OEDIPUS. What, did she give you it?

THEBAN.   She did, my lord.

OEDIPUS. With what intention?

THEBAN.   That I should destroy it.

OEDIPUS. Her own? – How could she?

THEBAN.   Frightened by
                                          oracles.   1130

OEDIPUS. What oracles?

THEBAN.   That it would kill its parents.

OEDIPUS. Why did you let it go to this man here?

THEBAN. I pitied it, my lord. I thought to send
    The child abroad, whence this man came. And he
    Saved it, for utter doom. For if you are
    The man he says, then you were born for ruin.

OEDIPUS. Ah God! Ah God! This is the truth, at last!
    O Sun, let me behold thee this once more,
    I who am proved accursed in my conception,
    And in my marriage, and in him I slew.   1140
             [*Exeunt severally* OEDIPUS, CORINTHIAN, THEBAN

Strophe 1

CHORUS. Alas! you generations of men!
(glyconics) Even while you live you are next to nothing!
    Has any man won for himself
    More than the shadow of happiness,
    A shadow that swiftly fades away?
    Oedipus, now as I look on you,
    See your ruin, how can I say that
    Mortal man can be happy?

Antistrophe 1

    For who won greater prosperity?
    Sovereignty and wealth beyond all desiring?   1150
    The crooked-clawed, riddling Sphinx,

87

Maiden and bird, you overcame;
You stood like a tower of strength to Thebes.
So you received our crown, received the
Highest honours that we could give –
King in our mighty city.

Strophe 2

Who more wretched, more afflicted now,
With cruel misery, with fell disaster,
Your life in dust and ashes?
    O noble Oedipus!   1160
    How could it be? to come again
A bridegroom of her who gave you birth!
How could such a monstrous thing
Endure so long, unknown?

Antistrophe 2

Time sees all, and Time, in your despite,
Disclosed and punished your unnatural marriage –
A child, and then a husband.
    O son of Laius,
    Would I had never looked on you!
I mourn you as one who mourns the dead.   1170
First you gave me back my life,
And now, that life is death.

Enter, from the palace, a MESSENGER

MESSENGER. My Lords, most honoured citizens of Thebes,
What deeds am I to tell of, you to see!
What heavy grief to bear, if still remains
Your native loyalty to our line of kings.
For not the Ister, no, nor Phasis' flood
Could purify this house, such things it hides,
Such others will it soon display to all,
Evils self-sought. Of all our sufferings   1180
Those hurt the most that we ourselves inflict.

CHORUS-LEADER. Sorrow enough – too much – in what was
                                                    known
  Already. What new sorrow do you bring?

MESSENGER. Quickest for me to say and you to hear:
  It is the Queen, Iocasta – she is dead.

CHORUS-LEADER. Iocasta, dead? But how? What was the cause?

MESSENGER. By her own hand. Of what has passed, the worst
  Cannot be yours: that was, to see it.
  But you shall hear, so far as memory serves,
  The cruel story. – In her agony   1190
  She ran across the courtyard, snatching at
  Her hair with both her hands. She made her way
  Straight to her chamber; she barred fast the doors
  And called on Laius, these long years dead,
  Remembering their by-gone procreation.
  'Through this did you meet death yourself, and leave
  To me, the mother, child-bearing accursed
  To my own child.' She cried aloud upon
  The bed where she had borne a double brood,
  Husband from husband, children from a child.   1200
  And thereupon she died, I know not how;
  For, groaning, Oedipus burst in, and we,
  For watching him, saw not *her* agony
  And how it ended. He, ranging through the palace,
  Came up to each man calling for a sword,
  Calling for her whom he had called his wife,
  Asking where was she who had borne them all,
  Himself and his own children. So he raved.
  And then some deity showed him the way,
  For it was none of us that stood around;   1210
  He cried aloud, as if to someone who
  Was leading him; he leapt upon the doors,
  Burst from their sockets the yielding bars, and fell
  Into the room; and there, hanged by the neck,
  We saw his wife, held in a swinging cord.

He, when he saw it, groaned in misery
And loosed her body from the rope. When now
She lay upon the ground, awful to see
Was that which followed: from her dress he tore
The golden brooches that she had been wearing,   1220
Raised them, and with their points struck his own eyes,
Crying aloud that they should never see
What he had suffered and what he had done,
But in the dark henceforth they should behold
Those whom they ought not; nor should recognize
Those whom he longed to see. To such refrain
He smote his eyeballs with the pins, not once,
Nor twice; and as he smote them, blood ran down
His face, not dripping slowly, but there fell
Showers of black rain and blood-red hail together.   1230
    Not on his head alone, but on them both,
Husband and wife, this common storm has broken.
Their ancient happiness of early days
Was happiness indeed; but now, today,
Death, ruin, lamentation, shame – of all
The ills there are, not one is wanting here.

CHORUS-LEADER. Now is there intermission in his agony?

MESSENGER. He shouts for someone to unbar the gates,
And to display to Thebes the parricide,
His mother's – no, I cannot speak the words;   1240
For, by the doom he uttered, he will cast
Himself beyond our borders, nor remain
To be a curse at home. But he needs strength,
And one to guide him; for these wounds are greater
Than he can bear – as you shall see; for look!
They draw the bolts. A sight you will behold
To move the pity even of an enemy.

                The doors open. OEDIPUS *slowly advances*

CHORUS. O horrible, dreadful sight. More dreadful far

(These verses sung or chanted in a slow march-time.) Than any I
have yet seen. What cruel frenzy
Came over you? What spirit with superhuman leap   1250
Came to assist your grim destiny?
Ah, most unhappy man!
But no! I cannot bear even to look at you,
Though there is much that I would ask and see and hear.
But I shudder at the very sight of you.

OEDIPUS [*sings in the dochmiac rhythm*]. Alas! alas! and woe for my
misery!

Where are my steps taking me?
My random voice is lost in the air.
O God! how hast thou crushed me!

CHORUS-LEADER [*spoken*]. Too terribly for us to hear or see.   1260

OEDIPUS [*sings*]. O cloud of darkness abominable,
My enemy unspeakable,
In cruel onset insuperable.
Alas! alas! Assailed at once by pain
Of pin-points and of memory of crimes.

CHORUS-LEADER. In such tormenting pains you well may cry
A double grief and feel a double woe.

OEDIPUS [*sings*]. Ah, my friend!
Still at my side? Still steadfast?
Still can you endure me?   1270
Still care for me, a blind man?
[*speaks*] For it is you, my friend; I know 'tis you;
Though all is darkness, yet I know your voice.

CHORUS-LEADER. O, to destroy your sight! How could you bring
Yourself to do it? What god incited you?

OEDIPUS [*sings*]. It was Apollo, friends, Apollo.
He decreed that I should suffer what I suffer;
But the hand that struck, alas! was my own,
And not another's.
For why should I have sight.   1280
When sight of nothing could give me pleasure?

91

CHORUS. It was even as you say.

OEDIPUS. What have I left, my friends, to see,
   To cherish, whom to speak with, or
   To listen to, with joy?
   Lead me away at once, far from Thebes;
   Lead me away, my friends!
   I have destroyed; I am accursed, and, what is more,
   Hateful to Heaven, as no other.

CHORUS-LEADER [*speaks*]. Unhappy your intention, and
                              unhappy 1290
   Your fate. O would that I had never known you!

OEDIPUS [*sings*]. Curses on him, whoever he was,
   Who took the savage fetters from my feet,
      Snatched me from death, and saved me.
      No thanks I owe him,
      For had I died that day
   Less ruin had I brought on me and mine.

CHORUS. That wish is my wish too.

OEDIPUS. I had not then come and slain my father,
      Nor then would men have called me   1300
      Husband of her that bore me.
   Now am I God's enemy, child of the guilty,
   And she that bore me has borne too my children;
   And if there is evil surpassing evil,
      That has come to Oedipus.

CHORUS-LEADER. How can I say that you have counselled well?
   Far better to be dead than to be blind.

OEDIPUS. That what is done was not done for the best
   Seek not to teach me: counsel me no more.
   I know not how I could have gone to Hades   1310
   And with these eyes have looked upon my father
   Or on my mother; such things have I done
   To them, death is no worthy punishment.

92

Or could I look for pleasure in the sight
Of my own children, born as they were born?
Never! No pleasure there, for eyes of mine,
Nor in this city, nor its battlements
Nor sacred images. From these – ah, miserable! –
I, the most nobly born of any Theban
Am banned for ever by my own decree   1320
That the defiler should be driven forth,
The man accursed of Heaven and Laius' house.
Was I to find such taint in me, and then
With level eyes to look *them* in the face?
Nay more: if for my ears I could have built
Some dam to stay the flood of sound, that I
Might lose both sight and hearing, and seal up
My wretched body – that I would have done.
How good to dwell beyond the reach of pain!

    Cithaeron! Why did you accept me? Why   1330
Did you not take and kill me? Never then
Should I have come to dwell among the Thebans.

    O Polybus! Corinth! and that ancient home
I thought my father's – what a thing you nurtured!
How fair, how foul beneath! For I am found
Foul in myself and in my parentage.

    O you three ways, that in a hidden glen
Do meet: you narrow branching roads within
The forest – you, through my own hands, did drink
My father's blood, that was my own. – Ah! do you   1340
Remember what you saw me do? And what
I did again in Thebes? You marriages!
You did beget me: then, having begotten,
Bore the same crop again, and brought to light
Commingled blood of fathers, brothers, sons,
Brides, mothers, wives; all that there can be
Among the human kind most horrible!

    But that which it is foul to do, it is
Not fair to speak of. Quick as you can, I beg,
Banish me, hide me, slay me! Throw me forth   1350

93

Into the sea, where I may sink from view.
I pray you, deign to touch one so afflicted,
And do not fear: there is no man alive
Can bear this load of evil but myself.

CHORUS-LEADER. To listen to your prayers, Creon is here,
For act or guidance opportune; for he,
In your defection, is our champion.

Enter CREON

OEDIPUS. Alas! alas! How can I speak to him?
What word of credit find? In all my commerce
With him aforetime I am proven false.   1360

CREON. No exultation, Oedipus, and no reproach
Of injuries inflicted brings me here;
But if the face of men moves not your shame,
Then reverence show to that all-nurturing fire,
The holy Sun, that he be not polluted
By such accursèd sight, which neither Earth
Nor rain from Heaven nor sunlight can endure.
   Take him within, and quickly: it is right
His kinsmen only should behold and hear
Evils that chiefly on his kinsmen fall.   1370

OEDIPUS. In Heaven's name – since you cheat my expectation,
So noble towards my baseness – grant me this:
It is for you I ask it, not myself.

CREON. What is this supplication that you make?

OEDIPUS. Drive me at once beyond your bounds, where I
Shall be alone, and no one speak to me.

CREON. I would have done it; but I first desired
To ask the God what he would have me do.

OEDIPUS. No, his command was given in full, to slay
Me, the polluter and the parricide.   1380

CREON. Those were his words; but in our present need
It would be wise to ask what we should do.

OEDIPUS. You will inquire for such a wretch as I?

CREON. I will; for now *you* may believe the god.

OEDIPUS. Yes; and on you I lay this charge and duty:
Give burial, as you will, to her who lies
Within – for she is yours, and this is proper;
And, while I live, let not my father's city
Endure to have me as a citizen.
My home must be the mountains – on Cithaeron,   1390
Which, while they lived, my parents chose to be
My tomb: they wished to slay me; now they shall.
For this I know: sickness can never kill me,
Nor any other evil; I was not saved
That day from death, except for some strange doom.
My fate must take the course it will. – Now, for my sons,
Be not concerned for them: they can, being men,
Fend for themselves, wherever they may be:
But my unhappy daughters, my two girls,
Whose chairs were always set beside my own   1400
At table – they who shared in every dish
That was prepared for me – oh Creon! these
Do I commend to you. And grant me this:
To take them in my arms, and weep for them.
My lord! most noble Creon! could I now
But hold them in my arms, then I should think
I had them as I had when I could see them.
Ah! what is this?
Ah Heaven! do I not hear my dear ones, sobbing?
Has Creon, in his pity, sent to me   1410
My darling children? Has he? Is it true?

CREON. It is; they have been always your delight;
So, knowing this, I had them brought to you.

OEDIPUS. Then Heaven reward you, and for this kind service

Protect you better than it protected me!
    Where are you, children? Where? O come to me!
Come, let me clasp you with a brother's arms,
These hands, which helped your father's eyes, once bright,
To look upon you as they see you now –
Your father who, not seeing, nor inquiring,   1420
Gave you for mother her who bore himself.
See you I cannot; but I weep for you,
For the unhappiness that must be yours,
And for the bitter life that you must lead.
What gathering of the citizens, what festivals,
Will you have part in? Your high celebrations
Will be to go back home, and sit in tears.
And when the time for marriage comes, what man
Will stake upon the ruin and the shame
That *I* am to my parents and to you?   1430
Nothing is wanting there: your father slew
His father, married her who gave him birth,
And then, from that same source whence he himself
Had sprung, got you. – With these things they will taunt you;
And who will take you then in marriage? – Nobody;
But you must waste, unwedded and unfruitful.
    Ah, Creon! Since they have no parent now
But you – for both of us who gave them life
Have perished – suffer them not to be cast out
Homeless and beggars; for they are your kin.   1440
Have pity on them, for they are so young,
So desolate, except for you alone.
Say 'Yes', good Creon! Let your hand confirm it.
    And now, my children, for my exhortation
You are too young; but you can pray that I
May live henceforward – where I should; and you
More happily than the father who begot you.

CREON. Now make an end of tears, and go within.

OEDIPUS. Then I must go – against my will.

CREON. There is a time for everything.   1450

96

OEDIPUS. You know what I would have you do?

CREON. If you will tell me, I shall know.

OEDIPUS. Send me away, away from Thebes.

CREON. The God, not I, must grant you this.

OEDIPUS. The gods hate no man more than me!

CREON. Then what you ask they soon will give.

OEDIPUS. You promise this?

CREON.   Ah no! When I
Am ignorant, I do not speak.

OEDIPUS. Then lead me in; I say no more.

CREON. Release the children then, and come.   1460

OEDIPUS. What? Take these children from me? No!

CREON. Seek not to have your way in all things:
Where you had your way before,
Your mastery broke before the end.

(There was no doubt a short concluding utterance from the Chorus. What stands in the MSS. appears to be spurious.)

ELECTRA

DRAMATIS PERSONAE

ORESTES, *only son of Agamemnon and Clytemnestra*
PYLADES, *his friend (He has no speaking part)*
PAEDAGOGUS, *an old slave, personal attendant of Orestes*
ELECTRA, *daughter of Agamemnon and Clytemnestra*
CHRYSOTHEMIS, *her sister*
CLYTEMNESTRA
AEGISTHUS
CHORUS *of women of Mycenae*

Scene: Mycenae, in Argos, before the royal palace

The time of the action is some fifteen or twenty years after the return of Agamemnon from the Trojan War and his murder at the hands of Clytemnestra his wife, and Aegisthus his cousin and her paramour. The murderers have usurped Agamemnon's crown and estate. The date of the first production of the play is unknown: probably some time between 425 and 415 B.C. The events here enacted were dramatized, very differently, by Aeschylus in the Choephori *or* Libation-bearers, *and by Euripides in his* Electra. *These two plays are extant; so too are the* Orestes *and* Iphigeneia in Tauris *of Euripides, in which he developed his version of the myth.*

ELECTRA

Enter ORESTES, PYLADES *and the* PAEDAGOGUS, *with two attendants*

PAEDAGOGUS. Here is the land of Argos. From this place
    Your father Agamemnon led the Greeks
    To Troy. How many years have you been longing
    To see what now your eyes can look upon:
    The ancient city Argos, once the home
    Of Io and her father Inachus.
    Now look upon it: there, the market-place
    That bears Apollo's name, and to the left
    Is Hera's famous temple. The place where we
    Are standing now – my son, this is Mycenae,   10
    Golden Mycenae, and the blood-drenched palace
    Of Pelops' dynasty is here, the place
    From which your sister saved you, as a baby,
    When they had murdered Agamemnon. I
    Took you to safety, I have brought you up
    To manhood. Now you must avenge your father.
      So now, Orestes, you and Pylades
    Your loyal friend, resolve with no delay
    What you will do. For dawn has come; the stars
    Have vanished from the darkness of the sky;   20
    The birds are striking up their morning songs;
    People will soon be stirring. Little time
    Is left to you; the hour has come for action.

ORESTES. My friend, my loyal servant: everything
    You say or do proclaims your true devotion.
    Just as a horse, if he is thoroughbred,
    Will keep his mettle even in old age,
    Will never flinch, but in the face of danger
    Prick up his ears, so you are ever first
    To proffer help and to encourage me.   30

You then shall hear my plan, and as you listen
Give it your sharp attention, to amend
Whatever seems amiss.
I went to Delphi, and I asked Apollo
How best I might avenge my father's death
On those who murdered him. The god's reply
Was brief; it went like this: *Not with an army*
But with your own right hand, by stratagem,
Give them what they have earned, and kill them both.
Therefore, since this is what the god has said,   40
Your part shall be to have yourself admitted
Inside the palace when the moment favours.
Find out what is afoot; return to me
And tell me what you can. – They will not know you;
You have grown old, so many years have passed;
Your silver hair will keep them from suspecting.
Your story shall be this, that you have come
From foreign parts, from Phanoteus of Phokis –
For he is one of their most trusted allies;
Tell them Orestes has been killed, and give   50
Your oath that it is true: he met his death
Competing in the Pythian Games at Delphi,
Flung from his racing-chariot. Let this be
The tale. And for myself, the god commanded
That I should first go to my father's tomb
And pay my tribute with a lock of hair
And wine-libation. This then will I do;
And I will find the urn which you have told me
Lies hidden in a thicket, and with that
I will come back. This urn of beaten bronze   60
Shall bring them joy – though not for long; for it
(So we will tell them) holds the ash and cinders
Of this my body that the fire consumed. –
Why should I fear an omen, if I say that I
Am dead, when by this story I fulfil
My life's true purpose, to secure my vengeance?
No need to fear a tale that brings me gain.

For I have heard of those philosophers
Who were reported dead: when they returned,
Each to his city, they were honoured more.   70
And so, I trust, may I, through this pretence,
Look down triumphant like the sun in heaven
Upon my enemies.
Only do thou, my native soil; you, gods of Argos,
Receive and prosper me. House of my fathers,
Receive me with your blessing! The gods have sent me,
And I have come to purify and purge you.
Do not reject me, drive me not away,
But let me enter into my possessions;
Let me rebuild my father's fallen house.   80
    Such is my prayer. My friend, go to your task
And do it well. We go to ours; for Time
Calls only once, and that determines all.

ELECTRA [*within*]. Ah me! Ah me!

PAEDAGOGUS. Listen, my son: I thought I heard a cry
  From near the gates, a cry of bitter grief.

ORESTES. Electra, my unhappy sister! Could
  It be her cry? – Let us wait and listen.

PAEDAGOGUS. No. The command that God has given us,
  That must come first, to offer your libations   90
  At Agamemnon's tomb. His aid will bring
  Victory to us, and ruin to his foes.
    [*Exeunt* ORESTES, PYLADES, *the* PAEDAGOGUS, *and attendants*

Enter ELECTRA

ELECTRA.   Thou holy light,
(anapaests: chanted) Thou sky that art earth's canopy,
  How many bitter cries of mine
  Have you not heard, when shadowy night
  Has given place to days of mourning!
  And when the night has come again
  My hateful bed alone can tell
  The tears that I have shed within   100

103

This cruel palace. O my father!
No Trojan spear, no god of war,
Brought death to you on foreign soil.
My mother killed you, and her mate
Aegisthus! As a woodman fells
An oak, they took a murderous axe
   And cut you down.
And yet no other voice but mine
Cries out upon this bloody deed. 110
I only, father, mourn your death.
   Nor ever will
I cease from dirge and sad lament
So long as I behold the sun
By day and see the stars by night;
But like the sorrowing nightingale
Who mourns her young unceasingly,
Here at the very gates will I
Proclaim my grief for all to hear.

You powers of Death! you gods below!
Avenging Spirits, who behold 120
Each deed of blood, each faithless act
Dishonouring the marriage-vow,
Desert me not. Come to my aid!
Avenge my father's death!
And send my brother; bring to me
Orestes! For I can no more
Sustain this grief; it crushes me.

Enter the CHORUS

Strophe 1

CHORUS. Electra, child of a most pitiless mother,
   Why are you so wasting your life in unceasing
   Grief and despair? Agamemnon 130
   Died long ago. Treachery filled the heart,
   Your mother's heart, that gave him,

Snared, entrapped, to a shameful supplanter who killed him.
    If I may dare to say it, may
    Those who did such a thing
    Suffer the same themselves.

ELECTRA. O my noble, generous friends,
    You are here, I know, to comfort me in my sorrow.
    Welcome to me, most welcome, is your coming.
    But ask me not to abandon my grief   140
        Or cease to mourn my father.
    No, my friends; give, as always you give me, your love and
                              devotion,
    But bear with my grief; I cannot betray my sorrow.

Antistrophe 1

CHORUS. But he has gone to the land to which we all must
    Go. Neither by tears nor by mourning can
    He be restored from the land of the dead.
    Yours is a grief beyond the common measure,
        A grief that knows no ending,
    Consuming your own life, and all in vain.
        For how can mourning end wrong?   150
    Cannot you part yourself from your long
        Sorrow and suffering?

ELECTRA. Hard the heart, unfeeling the mind,
    Of one who should forget a father, cruelly slain.
    Her will my heart follow, the sad nightingale,
        Bird of grief, always lamenting
        Itys, Itys, her child.
    And O, Niobe, Queen of Sorrow, to thee do I turn, as a
                              goddess
    Weeping for ever, in thy mountain-tomb.

Strophe 2

CHORUS.   Not upon you alone, my child,   160
    Has come the heavy burden of grief

That chafes you more than those with whom you live,
The two bound to you by kindred blood.
See how Chrysothemis lives, and Iphianassa,
    Your two sisters within.
    He also lives, your brother,
    Although in exile, suffering grief;
    And glory awaits Orestes, for
He will come by the kindly guidance of Zeus, and be
Received with honour and welcome, here in Mycenae.   170

ELECTRA. But I, year after year, waiting for him,
Tread my weary path, unwedded, childless,
Bathed in tears, burdened with endless sorrow.
For the wrongs he has suffered, the crimes of which I have
                                  told him,
He cares nothing. Messages come; all are belied;
He longs to be here, but not enough to come!

Antistrophe 2

CHORUS.   Comfort yourself, take comfort, child;
    Zeus is still King in the heavens.
He sees all; he overrules all things.
Leave this bitter grief and anger to him.   180
Do not go too far in hatred with those you hate,
    Nor be forgetful of him.
    Time has power to heal all wounds.
    Nor will he who lives in the rich
    Plain of Crisa, near the sea,
Agamemnon's son, neglect his own father.

ELECTRA. But how much of my life has now been spent,
Spent in despair! My strength will soon be gone.
I am alone, without the comfort of children; no
Husband to stand beside me, and share the burden;   190
Spurned like a slave, dressed like a slave, fed on the scraps,
I serve, disdained by all – in the house of my fathers!

Strophe 3

CHORUS.   Pitiful the cry at his return,
    Your father's cry in the banquet-hall,
When the straight, sharp blow of an axe was launched at him.
    Guile was the plotter, lust was the slayer,
    Hideous begetters of a hideous crime,
    Whether the hand that wrought the deed
Was a mortal hand, or a Spirit loosed from Hell.

ELECTRA. That day of horrors beyond all other horrors!   200
Hateful and bitter beyond all other days!
    That accursed night of banqueting
    Filled with fear and blood!
My father looked, and saw two murderers aiming
    A deadly, cowardly blow at him,
    A blow that has betrayed my life
    To slavery, to ruin.
    O God that rulest Heaven and Earth,
    Make retribution fall on them!
    What they have done, that may they suffer.   210
    Leave them not to triumph!

Antistrophe 3

CHORUS.   Yet you should be wise, and say no more.
    It is yourself and what you do
That brings upon yourself this cruel outrage.
Your sullen, irreconcilable heart,
    Breeding strife and enmity,
    Adds to your own misery.
To fight with those that hold the power is folly.

ELECTRA. I know, I know my bitter and hateful temper;
But see what I have to suffer! That constrains me.   220
    Because of that, I cannot help
    But give myself to frenzied hate
So long as life shall last. My gentle friends,
    What words of comfort or persuasion

Can prevail, to reconcile
My spirit with this evil?
No; leave me, leave me; do not try.
These are ills past remedy.
Never shall I depart from sorrow
And tears and lamentation.   230

Epode

CHORUS. In love and friendship, like a mother,
  I beg you: do not make, my child,
    Trouble on top of trouble.

ELECTRA. In what I suffer, is there moderation?
  To be neglectful of the dead, can that be right?
  Where among men is that accounted honour?
    I'll not accept praise from them!
    Whatever happiness is mine,
  I'll not enjoy dishonourable ease,
    Forget my grief, or cease to pay   240
    Tribute of mourning to my father.
  For if the dead shall lie there, nothing but dust and ashes,
  And they who killed him do not suffer death in return,
    Then, for all mankind,
  Fear of the gods, respect for men, have vanished.

CHORUS-LEADER. Your cause I make my own. So, if my words
  Displease you, I recall them and let yours
  Prevail; for I will always follow you.

ELECTRA. My friends, these lamentations are a sore
  Vexation to you, and I am ashamed.   250
  But bear with me: I can do nothing else.
  What woman would not cry to Heaven, if she
  Had any trace of spirit, when she saw
  Her father suffering outrage such as I
  Must look on every day – and every night?
  And it does not decrease, but always grows
  More insolent. There is my mother: she,

My mother! has become my bitterest enemy.
And then, I have to share my house with those
Who murdered my own father; I am ruled   260
By them, and what I get, what I must do
Without, depends on them. What happy days,
Think you, mine are, when I must see Aegisthus
Sitting upon my father's throne, wearing
My father's robes, and pouring his libations
Beside the hearth-stone where they murdered him?
And I must look upon the crowning outrage,
The murderer lying in my father's bed
With my abandoned mother – if I must
Call her a mother who dares sleep with him!   270
She is so brazen that she lives with that
Defiler; vengeance from the gods is not
A thought that frightens her! As if exulting
In what she did she noted carefully
The day on which she treacherously killed
My father, and each month, when that day comes,
She holds high festival and sacrifices
Sheep to the Gods her Saviours. I look on
In misery, and weep with breaking heart.
This cruel mockery, her Festival   280
Of Agamemnon, is to me a day
Of bitter grief – and I must grieve alone.
And then, I cannot even weep in peace:
This noble lady bids me stop, reviles
Me bitterly: 'You god-forsaken creature!
You hateful thing! Are you the only one
Who ever lost a father? Has none but you
Ever worn black? A curse upon you! May
The gods of Hades give you ample cause
To weep for evermore!' – So she reviles me.   290
But when she hears from someone that Orestes
May come, she flies into a frenzied rage,
Stands over me and screams: 'It's you I have
To thank for this, my girl! This is your work!

109

You stole Orestes from my hands, and sent
Him secretly away. But let me tell you,
I'll make you pay for this as you deserve.'
So, like a dog, she yelps, encouraged by
That glorious bridegroom who stands at her side,
That milksop coward, that abomination,   300
That warrior who shelters behind women.
   My cry is for Orestes and his coming
To put an end to this. O, I am sick
At heart from waiting; he is holding back,
And his delay has broken all my hopes.
Enduring this, my friends, how can I follow
Wisdom and piety? Among such evils
How can my conduct not be evil too?

CHORUS-LEADER. Come, tell me: is Aegisthus here, that you
   Say this to us, or is he gone from home?   310

ELECTRA. If he were here, I'd not have dared to come
   Outside the palace. No, he's in the country.

CHORUS-LEADER. If that is so, why then, I might perhaps
   Myself be bold, and speak with you more freely.

ELECTRA. Say what you will; Aegisthus is not here.

CHORUS-LEADER. Then tell me of your brother: is there news
   That he is coming, or is he still waiting?

ELECTRA. He promises – and that is all he does.

CHORUS-LEADER. So great an enterprise is not done quickly.

ELECTRA. Yet I was quick enough when I saved him!   320

CHORUS-LEADER. He'll not desert his friends. Have confidence.

ELECTRA. I have. If I had not I should have died.

CHORUS-LEADER. Hush, say no more! Chrysothemis is coming,
   Your sister, from the palace, carrying
   Grave-offerings, that are given to the dead.

110

CHRYSOTHEMIS. Why have you come again outside the gate,
    Spreading your talk? O, will you never learn?
    Will nothing teach you? Why do you indulge
    This vain resentment? I am sure of this:
    Mine is as great as yours. If I could find   330
    The power, they soon would learn how much I hate them.
    But we are helpless; we should ride the storm
    With shortened sail, not show our enmity
    When we are impotent to do them harm.
    Will you not do the same? The right may lie
    On your side, not on mine, but since *they* rule,
    I must submit, or lose all liberty.

ELECTRA. Shameful! that you, the child of such a father
    Should have no thought for him, but only for
    Your mother! All the wise advice you give me   340
    You learn of her; none of it is your own.
    But you must make your choice: to be a fool,
    Like me, or to be prudent, and abandon
    Those dearest to you. If you had the power,
    You say, you'd show them how you hate them both –
    And yet when I do all I can to avenge
    Our father, do you help me? No; you try
    To thwart me, adding cowardice on top
    Of misery. Come, tell me – or let me
    Tell you: if I give up my grief, what should   350
    I gain? Do I not live? Barely, I know,
    But well enough for me; and I give *them*
    Continual vexation, and thereby
    Honour the dead, if there is any feeling
    Beyond the grave. You hate them, so you tell me:
    Your tongue may hate them; what you do supports
    Our father's enemies and murderers.
    I will not yield to them, no, not for all
    The toys and trinkets that give you such pleasure.
    Enjoy your luxuries, your delicate food!   360

It is enough for me if I may eat
What does not turn my stomach. I have no
Desire to share in your high privileges.
And you would scorn them, if you knew your duty.
You might be known as Agamemnon's child,
But let them call you Clytemnestra's daughter,
And recognize your treason, who abandon
Your murdered father and your family.

CHORUS-LEADER. Do not give way to anger. Each of you
Can with advantage listen to the other.   370

CHRYSOTHEMIS. I am well used to her tirades, my friends;
I would not have provoked her, but that I
Know that the gravest danger threatens her:
They are resolved to end her long complaints.

ELECTRA. What is this awful thing? If it is worse
Than *this* I will not say another word.

CHRYSOTHEMIS. I'll tell you everything I know. – They have
                                                  determined,
If you will not give up these protestations,
To imprison you in such a place that you
Will never see the sun again, but live   380
To sing your own laments in some dark dungeon.
So think on this, or, when the blow has fallen,
Do not blame me. Now is the time for prudence.

ELECTRA. Will they do *that* to me?

CHRYSOTHEMIS.   They will; it is
Decreed, the moment that Aegisthus has returned.

ELECTRA. Then let him come at once, for all I care!

CHRYSOTHEMIS. How can you say it? Are you mad?

ELECTRA.   At least,
I shall be out of sight of all of you.

CHRYSOTHEMIS. But to give up the life you lead with us!

ELECTRA. A marvellous existence! One to envy!   390

CHRYSOTHEMIS. It could be, if you would behave with sense.

ELECTRA. You'll not teach *me* to abandon those I love.

CHRYSOTHEMIS. Not that, but to give in to those who rule us.

ELECTRA. Let that be your excuse; I will not make it!

CHRYSOTHEMIS. It is a duty, not to fall through folly.

ELECTRA. I'll fall, if fall I must, avenging *him*.

CHRYSOTHEMIS. Our father will not blame me, I am sure.

ELECTRA. Only a coward would rely on that!

CHRYSOTHEMIS. Will you not listen, and let me persuade you?

ELECTRA. Never! I hope my judgement will not fall   400
As low as that.

CHRYSOTHEMIS.   Then I will say no more.
I'll leave you now, and go upon my errand.

ELECTRA. Where are you going, with those offerings?

CHRYSOTHEMIS. I am to lay them on our father's tomb;
Our mother sent me.

ELECTRA.   She? Give offerings
To him who is her deadliest enemy?

CHRYSOTHEMIS. Say next: 'The husband slain by her own hand'!

ELECTRA. Who thought of this? Or who persuaded her?

CHRYSOTHEMIS. She had a dream, I think, that frightened her.

ELECTRA. Gods of our race! Be with us now, at last!   410

CHRYSOTHEMIS. Do you find cause of hope in this bad dream?

ELECTRA. Tell me the dream, and then perhaps I'll know.

CHRYSOTHEMIS. I cannot tell you much.

ELECTRA.   But tell me *that*!
The safety or the ruin of a house
Will often turn upon a little thing.

CHRYSOTHEMIS. They say that in her dream she saw our father
Returned to life and standing at her side;
He took the sceptre which he used to hold
Himself – the one that now Aegisthus carries –   420
And planted it beside the hearth; from that
There grew, and spread, an over-arching tree
That gave its shelter to the whole of Argos.
At sunrise, to allay her fear, she told
Her vision to the sun-god: one who stood
Nearby and heard reported it to me.
I cannot tell you more, except that I
Am sent because the dream has frightened her.

So now, I beg you, in the name of all
The gods we worship, do as I advise: 430
Give up this folly which will be your ruin.
If you reject me now, you will return
To me when nothing I can do will help you.

ELECTRA. Dear sister, do not let these offerings
Come near his tomb; it is a thing that law
And piety forbid, to dedicate
To him gifts and libations that are sent
By her, his deadliest, bitterest enemy.
Bury them in the ground, or throw them to
The random winds, that none of them may reach him.   440
No; let them all be kept in store for her
In Hell, a treasure for her when she dies.
If she were not the most insensate woman
The world has ever seen, she'd not have dared
To try to crown the tomb of him she killed
With gifts inspired by enmity. Think: would they
Cause any gratitude in him? Did she not kill him?
And with such hatred, and with such dishonour,
That she attacked even his lifeless body

And mangled it? You cannot think that gifts 450
Will gain her absolution from her crime?
Impossible! No, let them be, and make
A different offering at our father's grave:
Give him a lock of hair for token, one
Of yours, and one of mine – no lordly gifts,
But all I have; and give him too this girdle,
Poor, unadorned; and as you give them, kneel
Upon his grave; beseech him, from the world
Below, to look with favour on us, and
To give his aid against our enemies; 460
And that his son Orestes may be saved
To come in triumph and to trample on
His foes, that in the days to come we may
Grace him with gifts more splendid far than those
That we can offer now. For I believe,
I do believe, that in this dream, to her
So terrifying, the spirit of our father
Has played some part. However that may be,
My sister, do this service to yourself,
To me, and to the one we love beyond 470
All others, him who now is dead – our father.

CHORUS-LEADER. My child, if you are wise, you will do all
    She bids you, for she speaks in piety.

CHRYSOTHEMIS. Do it I will; when duty's clear, there is
    No cause to argue, but to do it quickly.
    But, O my friends, I beg you, keep it secret,
    This that I undertake. If it should come
    To Clytemnestra's knowledge, then I fear
    I should pay dearly for this enterprise.

[*Exit* CHRYSOTHEMIS

Strophe 1

CHORUS. If I have any foresight, any judgement to be trusted, 480
    Retribution is at hand; her shadow falls before she comes.

She is coming, and she brings with her a power invincible.
  Confidence rises in my heart;
  The dream is good; it makes me glad.
The King, your father, is not sunk in dull forgetfulness,
Nor does the rusty two-edged axe forget the foul blow.

Antistrophe 1

She will come swiftly and strongly, springing on them from an
                                                          ambush,
The Vengeance of the gods, coming in might. For they were
                                                           swept
By a passion for a lawless and bloody mating into crime.
  Therefore I feel glad confidence;   490
  The omen has not come in vain.
For evil doers must pay. Oracles and prophecies
Only deceive, if this dream is not now fulfilled.

Epode

That chariot-race of Pelops
Has become the cause of sorrow
And of suffering without end.
Since Myrtilus was thrown from
His golden car, and dashed to death into
The sea that roared beneath him,   500
Cruel violence and bloodshed
Have been quartered on this house.

Enter CLYTEMNESTRA, *with a servant carrying
materials for a sacrifice*

CLYTEMNESTRA. At large again, it seems – because Aegisthus
Is not at home to stop you. So you go
Roaming about, putting us all to shame!
But in *his* absence, you are not afraid
Of me! And yet you say to everyone
That I am cruel and tyrannical,
That I heap outrage both on you and yours.

116

I do no outrage; if my tongue reviles you,   510
It is because my tongue must answer yours.
Your father: that is always your excuse,
That he was killed by me. – By me! Of course;
I know he was, and I do not deny it –
Because his own crime killed him, and not I
Alone. And you, if you had known your duty,
Ought to have helped, for I was helping Justice.
This father of yours, whom you are always mourning,
Had killed your sister, sacrificing her
To Artemis, the only Greek who could endure   520
To do it – though his part, when he begot her,
Was so much less than mine, who bore the child.
So tell me why, in deference to whom,
He sacrificed her? For the Greeks, you say?
What right had they to kill a child of mine?
But if you say he killed *my* child to serve
His brother Menelaus, should not he
Pay me for that? Did not this brother have
Two sons, and should they rather not have died,
The sons of Helen who had caused the war   530
And Menelaus who had started it?
Or had the god of death some strange desire
To feast on mine, and not on Helen's children?
Or did this most unnatural father love
His brother's children, not the one I bore him?
Was not this father monstrous, criminal?
You will say No, but I declare he was,
And so would she who died – if she could speak.
Therefore at what has happened I am not
Dismayed; and if you think me wrong, correct   540
Your own mistakes before you censure mine.

ELECTRA. This time at least you will not say that I
      Attacked you first, and then got such an answer.
      If you allow it, I'll declare the truth
      On his behalf and on my sister's too.

CLYTEMNESTRA. I do allow it. Had you always spoken
  Like this, you would have given less offence.

ELECTRA. Then listen. You admit you killed my father:
  Justly or not, could you say anything
  More foul? But I can prove to you it was   550
  No love of Justice that inspired the deed,
  But the suggestions of that criminal
  With whom you now are living. Go and ask
  The Huntress Artemis why she becalmed
  The fleet at windy Aulis. – No; *I* will tell you;
  We may not question gods.
  My father once, they tell me, hunting in
  A forest that was sacred to the goddess,
  Started an antlered stag. He aimed, and shot it,
  Then made a foolish boast, of such a kind   560
  As angered Artemis. Therefore she held up
  The fleet, to make my father sacrifice
  His daughter to her in requital for
  The stag he'd killed. So came the sacrifice:
  The Greeks were prisoners, they could neither sail
  To Troy nor go back home; and so, in anguish,
  And after long refusal, being compelled,
  He sacrificed her. It was not to help
  His brother. But even had it been for that,
  As you pretend, what right had you to kill him?   570
  Under what law? Be careful; if you set
  This up for law, *Blood in return for blood*,
  You may repent it; you would be the first
  To die, if you were given your deserts.
  But this is nothing but an empty pretext;
  For tell me – if you will – why you are doing
  What is of all things most abominable.
  You take the murderer with whose help you killed
  My father, sleep with him and bear him children;
  Those born to you before, in lawful wedlock,   580
  You have cast out. Is this to be applauded?

Will you declare this too is retribution?
You'll not say that; most shameful if you do –
Marrying enemies to avenge a daughter!
But there, one cannot even warn you, for
You shout aloud that I revile my mother.
You are no daughter's *mother*, but a slave's
Mistress to me! You and your paramour
Enforce on me a life of misery.
Your son Orestes, whom you nearly killed,   590
Is dragging out a weary life in exile.
You say I am sustaining him that he
May come as an avenger: would to God
I were! Go then, denounce me where you like –
Unfilial, disloyal, shameless, impudent.
I may be skilled in all these arts; if so,
I am at least a credit to my mother!

CHORUS-LEADER. She is so furious that she is beyond
   All caring whether she be right or wrong.

CLYTEMNESTRA. Then why should I care what I say to her,   600
   When she so brazenly insults her mother,
   At her age too? She is so impudent
   That there is nothing that she would not do.

ELECTRA. Then let me tell you, though you'll not believe it:
   I *am* ashamed at what I do; I hate it.
   But it is forced on me, despite myself,
   By your malignity and wickedness.
   Evil in one breeds evil in another.

CLYTEMNESTRA. You shameless creature! What I say, it seems,
   And what I do give you too much to say.   610

ELECTRA. 'Tis you that say it, not I. You do the deeds,
   And your ungodly deeds find me the words.

CLYTEMNESTRA. I swear by Artemis that when Aegisthus comes
   Back home you'll suffer for this insolence.

ELECTRA. You see? You give me leave to speak my mind,
   Then fly into a rage and will not listen.

CLYTEMNESTRA. Will you not even keep a decent silence
   And let me offer sacrifice in peace
   When I have let you rage without restraint?

ELECTRA. Begin your sacrifice. I will not speak   620
   Another word. You shall not say I stopped you.

CLYTEMNESTRA [to the servant]. Lift up the rich fruit-offering to
                                              Apollo

   As I lift up my prayers to him, that he
   Will give deliverance from the fears that now
   Possess me.
   Phoebus Apollo, god of our defence:
   Hear my petition, though I keep it secret;
   There is one present who has little love
   For me. Should I speak openly, her sour
   And clamorous tongue would spread malicious rumour   630
   Throughout the city. Therefore, as I may
   Not speak, give ear to my unspoken prayer.
   Those visions of the doubtful dreams that came
   When I was sleeping, if they bring good omen,
   Then grant, O Lord Apollo, that they be
   Fulfilled; if evil omen, then avert
   That evil; let it fall upon my foes.
   If there be any who, by trickery,
   Would wrest from me the wealth I now enjoy,
   Frustrate them. Let this royal power be mine,   640
   This house of Atreus. So, until I die,
   My peace untroubled, my prosperity
   Unbroken, let me live with those with whom
   I now am living, with my children round me –
   Those who are not my bitter enemies.
      Such is my prayer; accept it graciously,
   O Lord Apollo; give to all of us
   Even as we ask. And there is something more.
   I say not what it is; I must be silent;

120

But thou, being a god, wilt understand.   650
Nothing is hidden from the sons of Zeus.
A silence, while CLYTEMNESTRA *makes her sacrifice.*

Enter the PAEDAGOGUS

PAEDAGOGUS [*to the chorus-leader*]. Might I inquire of you if I have
                                                        come
  To the royal palace of the lord Aegisthus?

CHORUS-LEADER. You have made no mistake, sir; this is it.

PAEDAGOGUS. The lady standing there perhaps might be
  Aegisthus' wife? She well might be a queen!

CHORUS-LEADER. She is indeed the queen.

PAEDAGOGUS.   My lady, greeting!
  One whom you know – a friend – has sent me here
  To you and to Aegisthus with good news.

CLYTEMNESTRA. Then you are very welcome. Tell me first,   660
  Who is the friend who sent you?

PAEDAGOGUS.   Phanoteus
  Of Phokis. – The news is of importance.

CLYTEMNESTRA. Then sir, what is it? Tell me. Coming from
  So good a friend, the news, I'm sure, is good.

PAEDAGOGUS. In short, it is Orestes. He is dead.

ELECTRA. Orestes, dead? O this is death to me!

CLYTEMNESTRA. What, dead? – Take no account of her.

PAEDAGOGUS. That is the news. Orestes has been killed.

ELECTRA. Orestes! Dead! Then what have I to live for?

CLYTEMNESTRA. That's your affair! – Now let me hear the
                                                truth,   670
  Stranger. What was the manner of his death?

PAEDAGOGUS. That was my errand, and I'll tell you all.

                          121

He came to Delphi for the Pythian Games,
That pride and glory of the land of Greece.
So, when he heard the herald's voice proclaim
The foot-race, which was first to be contested,
He stepped into the course, admired by all.
And soon he showed that he was swift and strong
No less than beautiful, for he returned
Crowned with the glory of a victory. 680
But though there's much to tell, I will be brief:
That man was never known who did the like.
Of every contest in the Festival
He won the prize, triumphantly. His name
Time and again was heard proclaimed: 'Victor:
Orestes, citizen of Argos, son
Of Agamemnon, who commanded all
The Greeks at Troy.' And so far, all was well.
But when the gods are adverse, human strength
Cannot prevail; and so it was with him. 690
For when upon another day, at dawn,
There was to be a contest of swift chariots,
He took his place – and he was one of many:
One from Achaea, one from Sparta, two
From Libya, charioteers of skill; Orestes
Was next – the fifth – driving Thessalian mares;
Then an Aetolian with a team of chestnuts;
The seventh was from Magnesia; the eighth
From Aenia – he was driving bays;
The ninth was from that ancient city Athens; 700
The tenth and last was a Boeotian.
They drew their places. Then the umpire set them
Each at the station that had been allotted.
The brazen trumpet sounded; they were off.
They shouted to their horses, shook the reins;
You could hear nothing but the rattling din
Of chariots; clouds of dust arose; they all
Were bunched together; every driver
Goaded his horses, hoping so to pass

His rival's wheels and then his panting horses.   710
Foam from the horses' mouths was everywhere –
On one man's wheels, upon another's back.
    So far no chariot had been overturned.
But now, the sixth lap finished and the seventh
Begun, the Aenian driver lost control:
His horses, hard of mouth, swerved suddenly
And dashed against a Libyan team. From this
Single mishap there followed crash on crash;
The course was full of wreckage. Seeing this,
The Athenian – a clever charioteer –   720
Drew out and waited, till the struggling mass
Had passed him by. Orestes was behind,
Relying on the finish. When he saw
That only the Athenian was left
He gave his team a ringing cry, and they
Responded. Now the two of them raced level;
First one and then the other gained the lead,
But only by a head. And as he drove,
Each time he turned the pillar at the end,
Checking the inside horse he gave full rein   730
To the outer one, and so he almost grazed
The stone. Eleven circuits now he had
Safely accomplished; still he stood erect,
And still the chariot ran. But then, as he
Came to the turn, slackening the left-hand rein
Too soon, he struck the pillar. The axle-shaft
Was snapped in two, and he was flung headlong,
Entangled in the reins. The horses ran
Amok into mid-course and dragged Orestes
Along the ground. O, what a cry arose   740
From all the company when they saw him thrown!
That he, who had achieved so much, should meet
With such disaster, dashed to the ground, and now
Tossed high, until the other charioteers,
After a struggle with the horses, checked them
And loosed him, torn and bleeding, from the reins,

123

So mangled that his friends would not have known him.
   A funeral-pyre was made; they burned the body.
Two men of Phokis, chosen for the task,
Are bringing home his ashes in an urn –   750
A little urn, to hold so tall a man –
That in his native soil he may find burial.
Such is my tale, painful enough to hear;
For those of us who saw it, how much worse!
Far worse than anything I yet have seen.

CHORUS-LEADER. And so the ancient line of Argive kings
   Has reached its end, in such calamity!

CLYTEMNESTRA. O Zeus! Am I to call this happy news,
   Or sorrowful, but good? What bitterness,
   If I must lose a son to save my life!   760

PAEDAGOGUS. My lady, why so sad?

CLYTEMNESTRA.   There is strange power
   In motherhood: however terrible
   Her wrongs, a mother never hates her child.

PAEDAGOGUS. So then it seems that I have come in vain.

CLYTEMNESTRA. No, not in vain! How can you say 'In vain',
   When you have brought to me the certain news
   That he is dead who drew his life from mine
   But then deserted me, who suckled him
   And reared him, and in exile has become
   A stranger to me? Since he left this country   770
   I have not seen him; but he charged me with
   His father's murder, and he threatened me
   Such that by day or night I could not sleep
   Except in terror; each single hour that came
   Cast over me the shadow of my death.
      But now . . . ! This day removes my fear of him –
   And her! She was the worse affliction; she
   Lived with me, draining me of life. But now
   Her threats are harmless; I can live in peace.

124

ELECTRA. O my Orestes! Here is double cause   780
  For grief: you dead, and your unnatural mother
  Exulting in your death! O, is it just?

CLYTEMNESTRA. You are not! He is – being as he is!

ELECTRA. Nemesis! Listen, and avenge Orestes.

CLYTEMNESTRA. She has heard already, and has rightly judged.

ELECTRA. Do outrage to me now: your hour has come.

CLYTEMNESTRA. But you will silence me, you and Orestes!

ELECTRA. Not now, alas! It is we that have been silenced.

CLYTEMNESTRA. My man, if you have stopped her mouth, you do
  Indeed deserve a very rich reward.   790

PAEDAGOGUS. Then I may go back home, if all is well?

CLYTEMNESTRA. Back home? By no means! That would not be
                                                  worthy
  Of me, or of the friend who sent you here.
  No, come inside, and leave this woman here
  To shout her sorrows – and her brother's too!
    [*Exeunt* CLYTEMNESTRA *and the* PAEDAGOGUS, *into the palace*

ELECTRA. What grief and pain she suffered! Did you see it?
  How bitterly she wept, how wildly mourned
  Her son's destruction! Did you see it? No,
  She left us laughing. O my brother! O
  My dear Orestes! You are dead; your death   800
  Has killed me too, for it has torn from me
  The only hope I had, that you would come
  At last in might, to be the avenger of
  Your father, and my champion. But now
  Where can I turn? For I am left alone,
  Robbed of my father, and of you. Henceforth
  I must go back again, for ever, into bondage
  To those whom most I hate, the murderers
  Who killed my father. O, can this be justice?
  Never again will I consent to go   810
  Under their roof; I'll lie down here, and starve,

125

Outside their doors; and if *that* vexes them,
Let them come out and kill me. If they do,
I shall be glad; it will be misery
To go on living; I would rather die.

COMMOS

Strophe 1

CHORUS. Zeus, where are thy thunderbolts?
(mainly in slow three-time) Where is the bright eye of the Sun-
　　God? if they look down upon this
　　　　And see it not.

ELECTRA.　　　　　*(An inarticulate cry of woe)*　　　　820

CHORUS. My daughter, do not weep.

ELECTRA.　　　　　*(Cry, as before)*

CHORUS. My child, say nothing impious.

ELECTRA. You break my heart.

CHORUS.　　　　　　　　But how?

ELECTRA. By holding out an empty hope.
　　Who now can avenge *him*?
　　His son Orestes is in his grave.
　　There is no comfort. O, let me be!
　　You do but make my grief the more.

Antistrophe 1

CHORUS. But yet, there was a king of old,　　　　830
　　Amphiareus: his wicked wife
　　Tempted by gold killed him, and yet
　　Though he is dead . . .

ELECTRA.　　　　　*(Cry, as before)*

CHORUS. He lives and reigns below.

ELECTRA.　　　　　*(Cry, as before)*

CHORUS. Alas indeed! The murderess . . .

126

ELECTRA. But she was killed!

CHORUS.   She was.

ELECTRA. I know! I know! Amphiareus
Had a champion to avenge him;   840
But I have none now left to me.
The one I had is in his grave.

Strophe 2

CHORUS. Your fate is hard and cruel.

ELECTRA. How well I know it! Sorrow, pain,
Year upon year of bitter grief!

CHORUS. Yes, we have seen it all.

ELECTRA. O offer not, I beg you,
An empty consolation.
No longer can I look for help
From my noble and loyal brother.   850

Antistrophe 2

CHORUS. Yet death must come to all men.

ELECTRA. But not like this! Dragged along,
Trampled on by horses' hooves!

CHORUS. No, do not think of it!

ELECTRA. O what an end! In exile,
Without a loving sister
To lay him in his grave, with none
To pay tribute of tears and mourning.

Enter CHRYSOTHEMIS

CHRYSOTHEMIS. Great happiness, dear sister, is the cause
Of my unseemly haste; good news for you,   860
And joy. Release has come at last from all
The sufferings that you have so long endured.

127

ELECTRA. And where can you find any help for my
   Afflictions? They have grown past remedy.

CHRYSOTHEMIS. Orestes has come back to us! I know it
   As surely as I stand before you now.

ELECTRA. What, are you mad, poor girl? Do you make fun
   Of your calamity, and mine as well?

CHRYSOTHEMIS. I am not mocking you! I swear it by
   Our father's memory. He is here, among us.   870

ELECTRA. You foolish girl! You have been listening to
   Some idle rumour. Who has told it you?

CHRYSOTHEMIS. No one has told me anything. I know
   From proof that I have seen with my own eyes.

ELECTRA. What proof, unhappy girl? What have you seen
   To be inflamed with this disastrous hope?

CHRYSOTHEMIS. Do listen, I implore you; then you'll know
   If I am talking foolishly or not.

ELECTRA. Then tell me, if it gives you any pleasure.

CHRYSOTHEMIS. I'll tell you everything I saw. When I   880
   Came near the tomb, I saw that offerings
   Of milk had just been poured upon the mound,
   And it was wreathed with flowers. I looked, and wondered;
   I peered about, to see if anyone
   Was standing near; then, as I seemed alone,
   I crept a little nearer to the tomb,
   And there, upon the edge, I saw a lock
   Of hair; it had been newly cut.
   Upon the moment, as I looked, there fell
   Across my mind a picture, one that I   890
   Have often dreamed of, and I knew that these
   Were offerings given by our beloved brother.
   I took them up with reverence; my eyes
   Were filled with tears of joy; for I was sure,
   As I am now, that none but he has laid

128

This tribute on the grave. Who else should do it
But he, or you, or I? It was not I,
That is quite certain. You have not been there;
How could you? Even to worship at a shrine
They do not let you leave the house, unpunished.   900
As for our mother, she has little mind
To make such offerings – and we should have known it.
No, dear Electra, they are from Orestes.
Therefore take courage! There is no such thing
As joy unbroken, or unbroken sorrow.
We have known sorrow – nothing else; perhaps
Today great happiness begins for us.

ELECTRA. O you unhappy girl! You little know!

CHRYSOTHEMIS. Unhappy? Is this not the best of news?

ELECTRA. The truth is very different from your fancy.   910

CHRYSOTHEMIS. This is the truth. Mayn't I believe my eyes?

ELECTRA. Poor girl! He's dead! We cannot look to him
For our deliverance; our hopes are gone.

CHRYSOTHEMIS. Alas, alas! . . . Who told you this?

ELECTRA. One who was there; a man who saw him killed.

CHRYSOTHEMIS. Where is the man? This fills me with dismay!

ELECTRA. At home; and, to our mother, very welcome.

CHRYSOTHEMIS. Alas, alas! Who could it then have been
Who put those many offerings on the tomb?

ELECTRA. It will be someone who has laid them there   920
As a memorial of Orestes' death.

CHRYSOTHEMIS. O, this is ruin! I came hurrying back,
So happy, with my news, not knowing this
Calamity. But all the woes we had
Before are with us still, and worse are added!

ELECTRA. Yet even so, if you will work with me,
We can throw off the weight that wears us down.

129

CHRYSOTHEMIS. What, can I bring the dead to life again?

ELECTRA. That's not my meaning; I am not a fool.

CHRYSOTHEMIS. Then what assistance can I give to you? 930

ELECTRA. I need your courage in a certain venture.

CHRYSOTHEMIS. If it will help us, I will not refuse.

ELECTRA. Remember: nothing prospers without effort.

CHRYSOTHEMIS. You may command whatever strength I have.

ELECTRA. This then is what I have resolved to do.
 You know, as I do, we have no support
 Of friends; of what we had we have been stripped
 By death. We two are left; we are alone.
 For me, while I had news about our brother,
 That he was well and strong, I lived in hope 940
 That he would some time come and punish those
 Who killed our father. Now that he is dead,
 I turn to you, that you will join your hand
 With mine, your sister's; help me, do not flinch:
 Aegisthus, who has murdered our dear father –
 We'll kill him! There's no reason now to keep
 It back from you. You cannot wait, inactive,
 Hoping for – nothing. What hope was left to you
 That is not shattered? This is what you have:
 Lasting resentment that you have been robbed 950
 Of all the wealth that rightly should be yours;
 Anger that they have let you live so long
 Unmarried – and do not think that this will change:
 Aegisthus is no fool; he can foresee,
 If you or I had children, they would take
 Revenge on him. Marriage is not for us.
 Therefore be with me in my resolution.
 This you will win: the praise of our dead father,
 And of our brother, for your loyalty;
 The freedom that is yours by right of birth; 960
 A marriage worthy of your station, since

130

All look admiringly upon the brave.
Do you not see what glory you will win
Both for yourself and me by doing this?
For all will cry, Argive or foreigner,
When they behold us: 'See! there are the sisters
Who saved their father's house from desolation;
Who, when their enemies were firmly set
In power, avenged a murder, risking all.
Love and respect and honour are their due;   970
At festivals and public gatherings
Give them pre-eminence, for their bravery.'
So we shall be acclaimed by everyone;
As long as we shall live our glory will
Endure, and will not fade when we are dead.

    My sister, give consent! Stand by your father,
Work with your brother, put an end to my
Calamities and yours; for to the noble
A life of shameful suffering is disgraceful.

CHORUS-LEADER. In such a case, in speech or in reply,   980
    Forethought and prudence are the best of helpers.

CHRYSOTHEMIS. Before she spoke at all, my friends, if she
    Had any prudence she might have preserved
    Some caution, not have thrown it to the winds.
    For what can you be thinking of, to arm
    Yourself with utter recklessness, and call
    On me to help you? Do you not reflect
    You are a woman, not a man? how weak
    You are, how strong your foes? that day by day
    Their cause grows stronger, ours diminishes   990
    And dwindles into nothing? Who can hope,
    Plotting to overthrow so powerful
    A man, not to be overwhelmed himself
    In utter ruin? Our plight is desperate
    Already; you will make it worse, far worse,
    If you are heard saying such things as this.
    It brings us nothing, if when we have won

That glorious repute, we die ignobly.
Mere death is not the worst; this is the worst,
To long for death and be compelled to live.   1000
No, I implore you, keep your rage in check
Before you bring destruction on us both
And devastation to our father's house.
What you have said shall be as if unsaid,
Of no effect; and you, before it is
Too late, must learn that since you have no strength
You have to yield to those that are in power.

CHORUS-LEADER. You must indeed. There is no better thing
For anyone than forethought and good sense.

ELECTRA. I had expected this; I thought that you   1010
Would spurn the offer that I made. And so
My hand alone must do it – for be sure,
It is a task that cannot be neglected.

CHRYSOTHEMIS. A pity you were not as bold as this
Before! You might have thwarted the assassins!

ELECTRA. I was too young to act. I had the will!

CHRYSOTHEMIS. Then try once more to be too young to act.

ELECTRA. It seems you are determined not to help me.

CHRYSOTHEMIS. Not in a venture that would be our ruin.

ELECTRA. How wise you are! And what a coward too.   1020

CHRYSOTHEMIS. Some day you'll praise my wisdom. I will bear it!

ELECTRA. I'll never trouble you so far as that!

CHRYSOTHEMIS. Who's wise, and who is foolish, time will show.

ELECTRA. Out of my sight! You are no use to me.

CHRYSOTHEMIS. I am, if you were wise enough to listen.

ELECTRA. Go to your mother; tell her everything!

CHRYSOTHEMIS. No; I refuse my help, but not from hatred.

132

ELECTRA. But in contempt! You make that very plain.

CHRYSOTHEMIS. Trying to save your life! Is that contempt?

ELECTRA. Am I to do what you imagine right?   1030

CHRYSOTHEMIS. Yes; and when you are right, I'll follow you.

ELECTRA. To be so plausible – and be so wrong!

CHRYSOTHEMIS. These are the very words I'd use of you.

ELECTRA. The right is on my side. Do you deny it?

CHRYSOTHEMIS. The right may lead a man to his destruction.

ELECTRA. That is no principle for me to follow.

CHRYSOTHEMIS. You'll think the same as I – when you have done
                                                            it.

ELECTRA. Do it I will. You shall not frighten me.

CHRYSOTHEMIS. Give up this folly! Be advised by me!

ELECTRA. No! There is nothing worse than bad advice.   1040

CHRYSOTHEMIS. Can I say nothing that you will accept?

ELECTRA. I have considered, and I have determined.

CHRYSOTHEMIS. Then I will go, since you do not approve
    Of what I say, nor I of what you do.

ELECTRA. Go then, for your ways never can be mine
    However much you wish. It is mere folly
    To go in quest of the impossible.

CHRYSOTHEMIS. If this, to you, is wisdom, follow it;
    But when it leads you to disaster, then
    At last you'll learn mine was the better wisdom.   1050
                                        [*Exit* CHRYSOTHEMIS

Strophe 1

CHORUS. We see the birds of the air, with what
    Sure instinct they protect and nourish

133

Those who brought them to life and tended them.
How can man disobey the laws of Nature?
The anger of the gods, the law established,
Enthroned in Heaven, will bring them retribution.
There is a Voice the dead can hear:
Speak, O Voice, to the King, to Agamemnon,
A message of shame and sorrow and deep dishonour.

Antistrophe 1

His house already was near to falling;   1060
Now a new cause of ruin threatens:
Discord comes to divide his champions.
Now no longer is daughter joined with daughter
In loyalty and love, but strife divides them.
Electra stands alone to face the tempest.
Never has she ceased to mourn,
Faithful, careless of life, if she may purge this
Palace of those two Furies, a foul pollution.

Strophe 2

He that is noble in spirit scorns
A life ignoble, darkened by shame,   1070
And chooses honour, my daughter,
As you chose to cleave to your father,
Accepting a life of sorrow.
Spurning dishonour, you have won a double fame:
Courage is yours, and wisdom.

Antistrophe 2

Still may I see you triumph, raised
Above your foes, restored to the power
And wealth of which they have robbed you.
You have known nothing but sorrow;
And yet by observing those great   1080
Laws of the gods, in piety and reverence,
You crown your sorrow with glory.

Enter ORESTES, PYLADES, *and attendants*

ORESTES. Ladies, we wish to know if we have been
Rightly directed to the place we look for.

CHORUS-LEADER. What is that you wish to find?

ORESTES.   Aegisthus,
If you could tell us where to find his palace?

CHORUS-LEADER. But it is here. You have been guided well.

ORESTES. Could one of you perhaps tell those within
That we have come, whom they have long awaited?

CHORUS-LEADER [*indicating* ELECTRA]. She best might do it; she is
                                    nearest to them.   1090

ORESTES. Madam, we are from Phokis; tell them, pray,
That we have certain business with Aegisthus.

ELECTRA. Alas, alas! You have not come with something
To prove it true – the rumour that we heard?

ORESTES. Of 'rumours' I know nothing. I am sent
By Strophius, Orestes' friend, with news.

ELECTRA. O, tell me what it is! You frighten me.

ORESTES. We bring him home; this little urn contains
What now is left of him; for he is dead.

ELECTRA. Ah, this is what I feared! I see your burden;   1100
Small weight for you, but heavy grief to me.

ORESTES. It is – if that which moves your sorrow is
Orestes' death: in *that* we bring his ashes.

ELECTRA. Then give it me, I beg you! If this vessel
Now holds him, let me take it in my arms.

ORESTES. Men, give it her, whoever she may be:
A friend; perhaps, one of his family.
This is no prayer of one who wished him evil.

135

ELECTRA. Orestes! my Orestes! you have come
    To this! The hopes with which I sent you forth   1110
    Are come to this! How radiant you were!
    And now I hold you – so: a little dust!
    O, would to God that I had died myself,
    And had not snatched *you* from the edge of death
    To have you sent into a foreign land!
    They would have killed you – but you would have shared
    Your father's death and burial; not been killed
    Far from your home, an exile, pitiably,
    Alone, without your sister. Not for you,
    The last sad tribute of a sister's hand!   1120
    Some stranger washed your wounds, and laid your body
    On the devouring fire; the charity
    Of strangers brings you home – so light a burden,
    And in so small a vessel!
                    O, my brother,
    What love and tenderness I spent on you!
    For you were my child rather than your mother's;
    I was your nurse – or you would not have had
    A nurse; *I* was the one you always called
    Your *sister* – and it has come to nothing.
    One single day has made it all in vain,   1130
    And, like a blast of wind, has swept it all
    To ruin. You are dead; my father too
    Lies in his grave; your death is death to me,
    Joy to our enemies: our mother – if
    She *is* a mother! – dances in delight,
    When you had sent me many a secret promise
    That you would come and be revenged on her.
    But no! A cruel fate has ruined you,
    And ruined me, and brought it all to nothing:
    The brother that I loved is gone, and in   1140
    His place are ashes, and an empty shadow.

O pity! pity, grief and sorrow!
How cruel, cruel, is your home-coming,
My dearest brother! I can live no longer.
O take me with you! You are nothing; I
Am nothing, now. Let me henceforward be
A shade among the shades, with you. We lived
As one; so now in death, let us be one,
And share a common grave, as while you lived
We shared a common life. O, let me die;   1150
For death alone can put an end to grief.

CHORUS-LEADER. Your father died, Electra; he was mortal:
So has Orestes died; so shall we all.
Remember this, and do not grieve too much.

ORESTES. What answer can I make to this? What *can*
I say? I must, and yet I cannot, speak.

ELECTRA. Sir, what has troubled you? Why speak like this?

ORESTES. Are *you* the Princess? Can you be Electra?

ELECTRA. I *am* Electra, though I look so mean.

ORESTES. To think that it has gone so far as this!   1160

ELECTRA. But why such words of pity over *me*?

ORESTES. – Treated so harshly and with such dishonour!

ELECTRA. Ill words well spoken, stranger – of Electra.

ORESTES. – How cruel! Kept unmarried, and ill-used!

ELECTRA. Sir, why do you look at me so fixedly,
And in such pity?

ORESTES.   Little did I know
My own unhappiness, how great it was.

ELECTRA. What words of mine have made you think of *that*?

ORESTES. No words; it is the sight of all you suffer.

ELECTRA. The sight of it? What you can see is nothing!   1170

137

ORESTES. How? What can be more terrible than this?

ELECTRA. To live, as I do, with the murderers.

ORESTES. What murderers? Who are these guilty men?

ELECTRA. My father's. – And they treat me as their slave!

ORESTES. But who has forced you to this servitude?

ELECTRA. She who has the name of mother – nothing else!

ORESTES. What does she do? Oppression? Violence?

ELECTRA. Violence, oppression, everything that's evil!

ORESTES. You have no champion? no one to oppose them?

ELECTRA. The one I had is dead: here are his ashes. 1180

ORESTES. A cruel life! How much I pity you.

ELECTRA. You are the only one who pities me!

ORESTES. I am the only one who shares your sorrow.

ELECTRA. Who are you? Can it be you are some kinsman?

ORESTES. Give back the urn, and I will tell you all.

ELECTRA. No, no, I beg you; do not be so cruel!

ORESTES. Do as I ask; you will do nothing wrong.

ELECTRA. It is all I have! You cannot take it from me!

ORESTES. You may not keep it.

ELECTRA.   O, my dear Orestes,
How cruel! I may not even bury you.   1190

ORESTES. Your talk of burial, your tears, are wrong.

ELECTRA. How is it wrong to mourn my brother's death?

ORESTES. You must not speak of him in words like these.

ELECTRA. Must I be robbed of *all* my rights in him?

ORESTES. You are robbed of nothing! *This* is not for you.

ELECTRA. Yes, if I hold Orestes in my arms!

ORESTES. This is Orestes only by a fiction.

ELECTRA. Then *where* is my unhappy brother's grave?

ORESTES. Nowhere. The living do not have a *grave*!

ELECTRA. My friend! What do you mean? 1200

ORESTES. I mean – the truth.

ELECTRA. My brother is *alive*?

ORESTES. If *I'm* alive!

ELECTRA. *You* are *Orestes*?

ORESTES. Look upon this ring –
Our father's ring. – Do you believe me now?

ELECTRA. O day of happiness!

ORESTES. Great happiness!

ELECTRA. It is *your* voice? – And have you come?

ORESTES. My voice,
And I am here!

ELECTRA. I hold you in my arms?

ORESTES. You do – and may we nevermore be parted.

ELECTRA. O look, my friends! My friends of Argos, look!
It is Orestes! – dead, by artifice, 1210
And by that artifice restored to us.

CHORUS-LEADER. To see him, and to see your happiness,
My child, brings tears of joy into my eyes.

Strophe

(ELECTRA *sings*, ORESTES *speaks*)

ELECTRA. My brother is here! the son of my own dear father!
You longed to see me, and now, at last,
You have found me! O, you have come to me!

139

ORESTES. Yes, I have come: but wait; contain your joy
   In silence; they will hear us in the palace.

ELECTRA.   O by the virgin-goddess, by Artemis,
   I despise them, those in the palace –   1220
   Women, useless and helpless!
   O, why should I fear them?

ORESTES. Remember: women may not be too weak
   To strike a blow. You have seen proof of it.

ELECTRA.   Ah me! The foul crime, that no
   Darkness can ever hide, that no
   Oblivion can wash away, no
   Power on earth remove.

ORESTES. All this I know; but we will speak of it
   When we can speak of it without restraint.   1230

Antistrophe

ELECTRA.   Each moment of time, now or to come, is time
   To proclaim aloud the abomination.
   At last, at last, I can speak with freedom.

ORESTES. You can; and yet, until the hour has come,
   By speaking freely we may lose our freedom.

ELECTRA.   How can I chain my tongue and repress my joy?
   Can I look upon you and be silent,
   Safe returned, my brother?
   It is more than I dared hope.

ORESTES. I waited long, but when the voice of God   1240
   Spoke, then I made no more delay.

ELECTRA.   O, this is joy crowning joy, if
   Heaven has brought you home to me!
   I see the hand of God
   Working along with us.

ORESTES. To stem your flood of joy is hard, but yet
   There is some danger in this long rejoicing.

140

Epode

ELECTRA.   So weary was the time of waiting!
     Now when you have come at last
     And all my sorrows have reached their end,   1250
     O, do not check my happiness.

ORESTES. Nor would I do it – but we must be prudent.

ELECTRA.   My friends, I heard my brother's voice,
     And I had thought
     That I would never hear his voice again:
     How could I restrain my joy?
     Ah, now I have you; I can look upon
     The well-loved face that I could not forget
     Even in darkest sorrow

ORESTES. How much there is to hear! – our mother's sin   1260
     And cruelty, that our ancestral wealth
     Is plundered, ravished, wantonly misused
     By that usurper. Yet our time is short
     And their misdeeds are more than can be told.
     But tell me what may help our present venture:
     Where can I hide, or where can I confront
     Our foes, to turn their laughter into silence?
     And see to this: our mother must not read   1270
     Our secret in your face. Conceal your joy
     When we go in; look sad, and mourn, as if
     The tale that you have heard were true. There will
     Be time enough to smile when we have conquered.

ELECTRA. My brother, what seems good to you shall be
     My law; your pleasure shall be mine, for mine
     Is nothing, except what you have brought to me,
     And to win all there is I would not cause
     A moment's pain to you, nor would that serve
     The favour of the gods, which now is with us.   1280
     Now as to what you ask. – You surely know
     Aegisthus is abroad, not in the palace;

But she is there, and you need have no fear
That she will see a look of happiness
Upon my face. The settled hatred which
I have for her will banish any smile.
I shall be weeping! – though my tears will be
Of joy at your return. My tears today
Flow in abundance; I have seen you dead,
And now alive. So strange the day has been   1290
That if our father came and greeted us
I should not think it was a ghost; I should
Believe it. Therefore, being yourself a miracle
In your return, command me as you will;
For had you died, had I been left alone,
I should myself have ventured all, and found
Glorious deliverance, or a glorious death.

ORESTES. Hush! I can hear the steps of someone coming
Out of the palace.

ELECTRA.   You are welcome, strangers.
Enter; the burden that you bring is such   1300
As no one could reject – and no one welcome.

Enter the PAEDAGOGUS, *from the palace*

PAEDAGOGUS. You reckless fools! What, have you got no sense?
Do you not care whether you live or die?
Are you demented? Don't you understand
The peril you are in? Not one that *threatens*;
No, it is here! Had I not stood on guard
Inside the door they would have known your plot
Before they saw you. As it is, I took
Good care of that. So, make an end of talk
And these interminable cries of joy.   1310
Go in; delay is dangerous at such
A moment. You must act, and make an end.

ORESTES. When I go in, how shall I find it there?

PAEDAGOGUS. All's well. Rely on this: they will not know you.

ORESTES. You have reported, then, that I am dead?

PAEDAGOGUS. I have; in their eyes you are dead and gone.

ORESTES. And are they glad? Or what have they been saying?

PAEDAGOGUS. We'll speak of that hereafter. All is well
    Within the palace – even what is shameful.

ELECTRA. In Heaven's name, who is this man, Orestes?   1320

ORESTES. Do you not know him?

ELECTRA.   I cannot even guess.

ORESTES. You know the man to whom you gave me once?

ELECTRA. Which man? What are you saying?

ORESTES.   The man by whom
    You had me secretly conveyed to Phokis.

ELECTRA. What, this is *he*? – the only one I found
    Remaining loyal at our father's murder?

ORESTES. That is the man; no need to ask for proof.

ELECTRA. How glad I am! Dear friend, to you alone
    The house of Agamemnon owes deliverance.
    How come you here? Can you be really he   1330
    That saved us both from all that threatened us?
    Come, let me take your hands, those faithful hands,
    My friend! How could I not have known you, when
    You came to bring me joy – but joy concealed
    In words of deadly grief? I'll call you father,
    Give you a daughter's greeting – for to me
    You are a father. How I hated you
    A while ago; how much I love you now!

PAEDAGOGUS. It is enough. Though there is much to tell,
    There will be many days and many nights   1340
    In which, Electra, you may tell it all.
      One word with you, Orestes, Pylades:
    This is your moment; now she is alone,

No men-at-arms are near. But if you wait,
Then you will have to face not only them,
But many more – men trained to use their weapons.

ORESTES. Pylades, there is no longer time for talk;
It seems the hour has come. So, let us go;
And as I go I give my reverence
To all the gods that stand before the house.   1350

> [ORESTES *enters the palace with* PYLADES, *praying
> before images on either side of the gate.* ELECTRA
> *goes to the altar where Clytemnestra's offerings are
> still visible*

ELECTRA. O Lord Apollo, listen to their prayers,
Be gracious to them! Listen too to mine!
How often have I been thy suppliant
Bringing what gifts I had; and therefore now,
Although my hands are empty, I beseech thee,
I beg thee, I implore thee, Lord Apollo:
Give us thy favour, help our purposes,
And show mankind what chastisement the gods
Inflict on those who practise wickedness.

> [*Exit* ELECTRA, *into the palace*

Strophe

CHORUS.   Look where the god of death makes his way,   1360
(*dochmiacs: swift tempo*) Fierce and implacable.
The Furies, champions of Justice,
Hounds of the gods, hot on the trail of crime,
    Have entered the palace.
    Before me rises a vision:
    Soon shall I see fulfilment.

Antistrophe

The minister of the gods, with stealthy foot,
    Ushered within the palace,
    The ancient home of his fathers,   1370

Holds in his hand a keen whetted sword,
  With Hermes to guide him,
To shroud his designs in darkness
And lead him straight to vengeance.

Enter ELECTRA

ELECTRA. My friends, keep silent; wait. It will not be
For long. Their hands are ready; soon they'll strike.

CHORUS-LEADER. What are they doing now?

ELECTRA.   She has the urn,
  Preparing it for burial; they are near her.

CHORUS-LEADER. And why have you come out?

ELECTRA.   To stand on guard;
  To give the warning if Aegisthus comes.   1380

CLYTEMNESTRA [*within*]. Ah . . . ! So many
  Murderers, and not a single friend!

ELECTRA. Someone inside is screaming. Do you hear it?

CHORUS-LEADER. I heard. . . . It makes me shudder; it is fearful.

CLYTEMNESTRA. Aegisthus! O where are you? They will kill me!

ELECTRA. There, yet another scream!

CLYTEMNESTRA.   My son, my son!
  Take pity on your mother!

ELECTRA.   You had none
  For him, nor for his father!

CHORUS [*sings*].   O my city! Ill-starred race of our kings!
  So many years a doom has lain on you: 1390
    Now it is passing away.

CLYTEMNESTRA. Ah! . . . They have struck me!

ELECTRA. Strike her again, if you have strength enough!

CLYTEMNESTRA. Another blow!

ELECTRA.   Pray God there'll be a third,
    And that one for Aegisthus!

CHORUS [*sings*].   The cry for vengeance is at work; the dead are
                                                stirring.
        Those who were killed of old now
        Drink in return the blood of those who killed them.

CHORUS-LEADER. See, they are coming, and the blood-stained arm
    Drips sacrifice of death. It was deserved.   1400

                Enter ORESTES *and* PYLADES

ELECTRA. How is it with you both?

ORESTES.   All's well, within
    The palace, if Apollo's oracle was well.

ELECTRA. Then she is dead?

ORESTES.   No longer need you fear
    Your mother's insolence and cruelty.

CHORUS-LEADER. Be silent! I can see Aegisthus coming.

ELECTRA. Stand back, Orestes.

ORESTES.   Are you sure you see him?

ELECTRA. Yes, he is coming from the town. He smiles;
    We have him in our hands.

CHORUS [*sings*].   Back to the doorway quickly! One
        Task is accomplished; may the second prosper too!   1410

ORESTES. It will. No fear of that.

ELECTRA.   Then, to your station.

ORESTES. I go at once.

ELECTRA.   And leave the rest to me.

CHORUS [*sings*].   Speak some gentle words to him
        That he may fall, unawares,
        Into the retribution that awaits him.

                            146

AEGISTHUS. They tell me that some men have come from Phokis
  With news about Orestes; dead, they say,
  Killed in a chariot-race. Where are these men?
  Will someone tell me? [*To* ELECTRA.] You! Yes, you should
                                                        know;
  It will have special interest for you!   1420

ELECTRA. I know. Of course I know. I loved my brother;
  How then should I make little of his death?

AEGISTHUS. Then tell me where these men are to be found.

ELECTRA. In there.
  They've won their way to Clytemnestra's heart.

AEGISTHUS. And is it true that they have brought this message?

ELECTRA. More than the message: they brought Orestes too.

AEGISTHUS. What, is the very body to be seen?

ELECTRA. It is; I do not envy you the sight.

AEGISTHUS. Our meetings have not always been so pleasant! 1430

ELECTRA. If this proves to your liking, you are welcome.

AEGISTHUS. I bid you all keep silence. Let the doors
  Be opened.

Enter, from the palace, ORESTES *and* PYLADES, *bearing the shrouded
body of* CLYTEMNESTRA

            Citizens of Argos, look!
  If there is any who had hopes in him,
  That hope lies shattered. Look upon this body
  And learn that I am master — or the weight
  Of my strong arm will make him learn the lesson.

ELECTRA. I need no teaching; I have learned, at last,
  That I must live at peace with those that rule.

AEGISTHUS. Zeus! Here is one laid low, before our eyes,   1440
  By the angry gods — and may no Nemesis

147

Attend my words, or I unsay them. – Now,
Turn back the shroud, and let me see the face.
It was a kinsman, and I too must mourn.

ORESTES. This you should do; it is for you, not me,
To look upon this face and take farewell.

AEGISTHUS. It is indeed for me, and I will do it. –
Call Clytemnestra, if she is at hand.

ORESTES. She is not far away; look straight before you.

[AEGISTHUS *takes the face-cloth from the body*

AEGISTHUS. God! What is this?

ORESTES.   Some stranger, frightening
                                                you?   1450

AEGISTHUS. Who are you, that have got me in your clutches
For my destruction?

ORESTES.   Have you not seen already?
Someone you thought was dead is still alive.

AEGISTHUS. Ah. . . . Now I understand. – You, who speak,
You are Orestes!

ORESTES.   You could read the future
So well, yet were so blind.

AEGISTHUS.   Ah. . . . You have come
To kill me! Give me time, a little time,
To speak.

ELECTRA.   No, by the gods, Orestes! No
Long speech from him! No, not a single word!
He's face to face with death; there's nothing gained   1460
In gaining time. Kill him at once! And when
You've killed him, throw the body out of sight,
And let him have the funeral he deserves.
Animals shall eat him! Nothing less than this
Will compensate for all that he has done.

148

ORESTES. Sir, come with me into the house; this is
No time for talk. My business is your life.

AEGISTHUS. Why to the house? If you are not ashamed
At what you do, then do it openly.

ORESTES. You shall not order me. Go in, and die   1470
On the same spot on which you killed my father.

AEGISTHUS. This house of Atreus must, it seems, behold
Death upon death, those now and those to come.

ORESTES. It will see yours; so much I can foresee.

AEGISTHUS. You did not get this foresight from your father!

ORESTES. You have too much to say; the time is passing.
Go!

AEGISTHUS. Lead the way.

ORESTES.   You must go before me.

AEGISTHUS. That I may not escape you?

ORESTES   That you may not
Be killed where *you* would choose. You shall taste all
The bitterness of death. – If retribution   1480
Were swift and certain, and the lawless man
Paid with his life, there would be fewer villains.

[*Exeunt* ORESTES, PYLADES, ELECTRA, AEGISTHUS

CHORUS.   Children of Atreus, now at last
Your sufferings are ended. You have won
Your own deliverance; now once more
Is the line of your fathers restored.

149

ON THE DANCE-RHYTHMS USED
BY SOPHOCLES

Here are offered a few comments on some of the dance-rhythms used by Sophocles in these three plays. After all, the Greek tragic dramatists were not poets only, but also composers and choreographers. We know nothing about their music and can make only indirect inferences about their dances, but this seems insufficient reason for taking no notice of them at all.

The Greek feeling for rhythm seems to have been more subtle than ours is. In music, certainly, we are recovering some of our earlier flexibility; no longer can we be cheerfully confident that if the first bar of a composition is in three-time, so will its successors be, at least until the next double bar; but in our dances regularity of beat, and therefore of movement, seems still to prevail. This is not true of Greek dances; some were regular, 'isochronous', others not.

The regular ones give us little difficulty. There are two kinds of rhythm in four-time: the dactyl and the anapaest. The dactyl is —◡◡ or — —, a crotchet and two quavers, as it were, or two crotchets; and the dancers took their step on the first beat of the bar. The anapaest is the reverse: ◡◡—, having as variants — — or —◡◡; two quavers and a crotchet, or two crotchets, or a crotchet and two quavers: the step was taken on the third of the four beats. Aristoxenus, our earliest authority in these matters, and by far the most sensible, observed that the dactylic rhythm 'falls', and therefore is a calm one, while the anapaest 'rises', and is therefore more energetic. (If Aristoxenus' book *On Rhythm* had survived intact, instead of in a few miserable fragments, Greek Lyric Metres would be a much less baffling subject than it is.)

It is at once obvious why the anapaest, not the dactyl, should have been the march-rhythm, also why it could accept a wider range of syllabic variety than the dactyl: its energy could assimilate the apparent dactyl –∪∪. Something else becomes apparent – and this is the justification for the present Appendix: we can see, in certain passages, why Sophocles used the one rhythm or the other, and thereby can add something, though it may not be much, to our appreciation of his drama. In the first stanza of the second ode in the *Antigone* (vv. 336–7 and 347–8 of the present translation) we see clearly, at least in the strophe, why he suddenly deserts his glyconics and writes two verses in dactyls: shall we say that he is suggesting an unrelenting persistence – or even monotony? Again, since the dactylic movement is, as Aristoxenus remarked, smooth and steady, we can readily understand why the movements of the Chorus (and of Electra too?) should be predominantly in this rhythm during the first four stanzas of the lyrical dialogue between the Chorus and Electra. Or we can look back to, and understand, the sudden introduction of two anapaestic verses at vv. 459–460 and 467–8 of the *Oedipus*. In other words, we can gain a distant glimpse of Sophocles the choreographer.

Of regular rhythms in triple time there are three kinds. First there is the trochaic: –∪, or –∪–∪, $\frac{3}{8}$ or $\frac{6}{8}$, according as we take the unit to be –∪ or –∪–∪; and this, as the sensible Aristoxenus pointed out, depends on the tempo, speed, ἀγωγή. Sophocles, unlike Aeschylus, did not use this rhythm very much. The reverse is the iambus, ∪–, or ∪–∪–, a rising rhythm, therefore more energetic than the trochaic. Then there are what the Greeks called the Ionic rhythms, $\frac{3}{4}$, whether ∪∪– –, rising, or – – ∪∪, falling. These, to my ear at least and apparently to Plato's too, seem to be, of their nature, slower: Plato damned them as langorous, debilitating. Whatever Plato may have thought, Sophocles uses them at the beginning of his Danae-ode (*Antigone* 917–922, with the antistrophe), and at the beginning of the first ode in the *Electra* (480–482). In each case, and for an obvious reason, after a few verses in this rhythm he changes to the much more energetic iambic. Similarly in the *Electra*: after the smooth dactylic rhythm mentioned above, the dance makes more and more use of iambics. These are effects that we can appreciate, if at all, only through our ears; Sophocles' audience could see as well as hear them.

These rhythms are familiar to us; the others are not. They are, however, part of the drama; therefore it is worth while to understand them as far as we can. We will consider only two: the glyconic and the dochmiac.

If we disregard merely syllabic variants, which are many, the glyconic takes one of three forms:

$$— \cup \cup — \cup — \cup —$$
$$— \cup — \cup \cup — \cup —$$
$$— \cup — \cup — \cup \cup —$$

Let us consider the second of these, which is the commonest. Thinking of each long note, or syllable, as the equivalent of two short ones, two pulses, we see at once that the phrase consists of twelve pulses – but they are not evenly disposed, as they would be in our music; they are neither four threes nor three fours. Alternatively, if we do divide them into four threes, we find that the first pair are in falling rhythm and the second pair in rising rhythm. The point may be put differently. We will assume – and Aristoxenus at least countenances the assumption – that in this phrase the dancers took two steps, on the first and third long notes, and that on the second and fourth the foot was raised. If the rhythm were regular, they would move on the first and the seventh of the twelve pulses; instead of that they move on the first and the eighth: in the middle of the phrase there is a certain momentary hovering, a reversal of the rhythm from rising to falling – which is precisely what Aristoxenus says: the rhythm goes κατ᾽ ἀντίθεσιν, 'in contrary motion'. In the other two forms of the glyconic this hovering, or reversal, occurs in a different part of the phrase; in the first, for example, it comes after the third pulse. Therefore we can see, though indeed only dimly, how this continual reversal at one of three points in the phrase would give a certain life and plasticity to the dance; one would say perhaps a certain gaiety, except that the glyconic is often used where gaiety is out of the question, as for example in the first six verses of the second ode in the *Antigone*. In the first ode of this play two glyconic stanzas alternate with passages in anapaests: now that we have considered these two contrasting rhythms in some detail we can turn back to the ode and form perhaps a slightly more definite impression, not indeed of what the dance looked like, but of what it was intended to *feel* like.

The other rhythm, the dochmiac, has a much more strongly marked unevenness. Its Greek name means 'aslant'. Syllabically, the simplest form of it is ◡––◡–; the variants can seem bewildering, but the rhythmic pattern is perfectly clear: eight pulses, divided not 4 + 4 but 3 + 5, the 3 being in rising rhythm. How the steps were disposed I would not care to say: it seems clear that one would be taken on the second pulse; presumably a second on the seventh. This evidently implies an impassioned movement, and in fact the dochmiac is found only in highly emotional passages, whether of grief or joy. Not infrequently, and very naturally, it is accompanied by other rhythmical figures either in (iambic) triple time or in five-time – for Greek dancers and singers took kindly to fives.

ON THE PRONUNCIATION OF GREEK NAMES

By tradition, we give Greek proper names a Latin spelling, and then pronounce them in the English way, with the stress accent natural to English, though observing for the most part the original distinction between long and short vowels. As a convention this is intelligible, but there is nothing sacrosanct about it. For example, the Greek name Kithairon is spelt Cithaeron and then pronounced something like Sitheerun, but if an actor or producer dislikes hissing, why should he not revert to something like the Greek form? The Greek Iokaste is traditionally spelt Jocasta and the first syllable is pronounced like Joe; it is because I find this a nasty sound that I have partially reverted to the Greek spelling, as also with the name Phokis. On the other hand, it would be silly to disguise the familiar Mycenae by saying Mykenae. In the following list, my circumflex accent denotes a long syllable; the acute accent marks the syllable which normally carries our English stress; it may be assumed that the vowel is short unless it has the circumflex accent. *Ch* should always be made hard, unless indeed an aspirated *k* (as in *loch*) is preferred. The diphthong *ae* is the Latinization of *ai*; pronunciation in English varies between a long *e* ('see') and *i* (as in *high*). Surely, so long as we are consistent, we are entitled to apply our ideas of euphony. *Oe* regularly becomes the long *e* (though not in America), and final *eus* rhymes with *deuce*.

Annotated List of Proper Names

Abae: an oracular shrine in Phokis.
Acheron: 'Lamentation': one of the rivers of the underworld.
Aetôlia (Eetólia: Ayetolia would be pedantic)
Agênôr: an ancient king of Tyre, father of Cadmus. (*g* hard)
Ámphiareús (stress on the first and fourth syllables)

Amphîôn: a mythical musician whose music raised the walls of Thebes.

Amphitrîtê: a sea-goddess.

Aulis (Awlis traditional, Owlis pedantic)

Boeôtia (Bee-ó-shya): the region in which Thebes was the largest city.

Chrysóthemis (stress on the second syllable; the *y* represents a long vowel, but the fact is commonly ignored)

Dêmêtêr: a goddess of vegetation, especially of corn.

Dircê (Dirke): a river near Thebes.

Dionŷsus

Eteoclês (the first three syllables are all short; some stress the first, some the second)

Haemôn (Heemon, Haymon, Highmon, are all possible pronunciations)

Hêlios: the Sun-god.

Iphianassa (stress on the first and fourth syllables)

Ismênus: a river near Thebes, and a local god.

Ister: the Danube.

Lábdacus

Menoeceus (Menoikeus may be preferred to Meneekeus or Meneeseus)

Meropê

Pélops (not Peelops)

Phánoteus

Polydôrus

Pýlades (Pill-a-dês; though one often hears Pighl-a-dês)

Pŷthô: the priestess at Delphi; also Delphi in general.

Erinys (plural: Erinyes): commonly rendered Furies or Avengers. These were the agents of Dike, which we translate as best we can: Justice, or Retribution, according to the context. Dike really means something like 'the way in which things regularly happen'; the Erinyes therefore punish or correct infringements of the established and proper order, whether in the moral or the physical universe. Thus in the *Iliad*, when Achilles' horse has spoken to him to warn him, it is the Erinyes which stop the horse's mouth.

SOME NOTES ON THE MYTHS

The story of the Pelopid dynasty, of the Curse in the House of Atreus, is too well known to need summarizing here. There are however three points in Sophocles' handling of it which may deserve brief comment: two of them illustrate the great freedom with which the Greek poets remodelled myth to suit their immediate purpose.

1. Aeschylus and Euripides both represent Orestes as being pursued by the Erinyes (Furies, Avengers) because of his killing of Clytemnestra; Sophocles' play not only contains no hint of such a pursuit; it actually makes the Erinyes, with Ares and Hermes, divine partners in the act of vengeance (vv. 1362–4). The reason is plain enough: Sophocles' theme is that a crime like that of Aegisthus and Clytemnestra will naturally, if not even inevitably, generate its own retribution; therefore he makes the divine powers – Zeus, Apollo, the Erinyes – favour those who are, in the nature of the case, seeking to avenge the crime and to reverse the lawless usurpation.

2. Sophocles' version of the sacrifice of Iphigeneia at Aulis is different from what Aeschylus had devised. Aeschylus made Artemis demand the sacrifice not because of something that Agamemnon had already done, but because of what he was proposing to do, namely to sacrifice lives in a 'war for a wanton woman': he may abandon his war and save his daughter, or he may kill his daughter, fight and win his war – and then return to face the retribution that awaits the man who has blood on his hands. Sophocles returns to what was in fact the traditional story, the incident of the stag; he also makes Artemis raise not adverse winds but no winds at all, so that the fleet could sail neither to Troy nor back home. Again the reason is clear: Sophocles wishes Agamemnon to be as guiltless as may be.

3. The earlier part of the myth, all that concerns Atreus and Thyestes, Sophocles naturally omits, as irrelevant to his theme; he does however, in his first ode, go back to an even earlier incident, 'the chariot-race of Pelops' – and one wonders why. The story, in brief, is as follows. Pelops ('Ruddy-face'), the founder of the dynasty, was a young hero from Asia Minor. He risked all in making a dangerous bid for the hand of Hippodameia, daughter of Oenomaus, king of Elis in the Peloponnesus, 'island of Pelops'; the terms were that any suitor had to run a chariot race with Oenomaus: if he won, the lady was his; if he lost, he was to be killed. Previous suitors had lost; Pelops won, either through his own skill and the aid of a god, or (in the version followed by Sophocles) by bribing Oenomaus' charioteer MYRTILUS to remove a linch-pin from Oenomaus' chariot so that the king was thrown out and killed. Myrtilus himself then offered insult to Hippodameia and was flung from a cliff into the sea by Pelops; but before he drowned he uttered a curse on Pelops. This was the beginning of the long chain of disaster in the Pelopid house. The reason why in this detail alone Sophocles harked back to the earliest part of the myth is presumably that in his play the vengeance taken by Orestes and Electra is going to square all accounts, with the restoration of the lawful heir; therefore he refers, thus briefly, to the beginning of all the trouble. Further, it is at least interesting to observe that the final triumph also involves a chariot race, though a fictitious one.

AMPHIARÄUS (or Amphiareus). There is a passing allusion to this hero in the Electra (vv. 830 ff.). He, a wise man and a prophet, was a brother-in-law to the king of Argos, Adrastus, who gave help to Polyneices in his attack on Thebes. Disapproving of the whole expedition, and knowing that it was doomed, Amphiaraus was reluctant to join it, but he was over-persuaded by his wife Eriphyle, whom Polyneices had bribed with a golden necklace. When the defeated Argives were in flight from Thebes the earth opened and swallowed Amphiaraus alive, with his chariot. It is for this reason that he is said, in the play, to be living and ruling in the underworld.

This, by successive accretions, became even more elaborate and no less sanguinary than the story of the Pelopids. So far as the *Tyrannus* is concerned it seems worth while only to mention some aspects of the myth which Sophocles conspicuously does *not* use. Aeschylus (apparently) represented that Laius, three times, was given a solemn warning by the god not to have a son, for a son of his would prove to be the ruin of the city. So also Euripides: he wrote a kind of chronicle-play on the House of Laius (*The Phoenician Women*) some ten or fifteen years after the *Tyrannus*, and in the prologue, spoken by Iocasta – who has not killed herself, as in Sophocles – we hear that Apollo had expressly warned Laius, but that he, 'giving way to pleasure, and in his cups', did nevertheless beget Oedipus. It is important therefore, if we are not to frustrate Sophocles, to notice that he does not represent this begetting as a wanton defiance of the god. Indeed the words that he writes for Iocasta are consistent with the sup-position that the child was conceived already: Jebb translates them: 'An oracle came to Laius once – I will not say from the god himself, but from his ministers – that the doom should overtake him to die by the hand of his child, who should spring from him and me.' Therefore, if we imagine that Laius was punished for disobedience, or for lust, or hybris, we are on the wrong track, so far as Sophocles is concerned. As he models the story, Laius– like his son after him – is expressly warned of a danger, takes resolute measures to avert it (for which Sophocles imputes no blame) – and fails.

The *Antigone* is the most lyrical of the three plays, and perhaps for that reason ranges more widely in myth.

The Thebans are 'the offspring of a Dragon': this is a refer-ence to the story of Cadmus, the founder of the city and the dynasty. He, an immigrant from Phoenicia, was led by a cow to the spot divinely appointed to be the site of his city. There he was incommoded by a dragon, which he killed; then, on divine prompting, he sowed the teeth of the dragon, and from them instantly sprang up a company of armed men, who became the ancestors of the Theban race. A later echo of the same story is referred to, rather mysteriously so far as we are concerned, by Sophocles in his account of Eurydice's suicide: she, with her last breath, 'lamented MEGAREUS who was slain of old', and leaves her curse on Creon, 'slayer of his son(s)' – for the word used here could mean either. Our earliest extant version of this story is in *The Phoenissae* of Euripides, thirty years later than the *Antigone*. Euripides gives it a distinctly melodramatic turn: the Argive army is already besieging Thebes, and Teiresias informs Creon that the city can survive only by the sacrifice of one of 'the sown men', i.e. the direct descendants of the dragon's teeth. There exist only two, other than Creon: Haemon and Menoeceus (whom Sophocles calls Megareus). Creon must sacrifice one of them: not Haemon, for he is married, therefore Menoeceus. Creon refuses, but Menoeceus nobly kills himself to save the city. This is certainly not the form of the story that Sophocles had in mind and expected his audience to recall: what that form was, we cannot tell.

Three separate myths are used in the fifth ode of the *Antigone*. DANAE was the daughter of an Argive king Acrisius. He received a warning rather like the one that came to Laius: if his daughter had a son, that son would kill him. It was to avert this that he imprisoned Danae in a tower; but Zeus came to her in the form of golden rain (interpreted by some modern Higher Critic to mean bribery of Danae's gaoler), and she bore Perseus, the one who slew the Gorgon and, after many other adventures, Acrisius himself, thus fulfilling the oracle.

LYCURGUS was a king in Thrace, the wild North – a parallel to Pentheus in *The Bacchae*, who bitterly opposed the introduction of Dionysiac worship in Thebes and was in consequence torn to pieces by the Bacchants, one of whom was his own mother. Lycurgus did the same. To punish him Dionysus drove him mad; in which condition he did many wild things, until his people shut him up in a cave. He too met his death by being torn to pieces, though by animals.

PHINEUS' two sons had as mother a certain Cleopatra, daughter of an Athenian princess Oreithyia whom Boreas the North Wind had carried off to Thrace from her home on the Acropolis.

Cleopatra's husband Phineus was king in Salmydessus, on the coast of the Black Sea, but he set her aside, and imprisoned her, in order to marry Eidothea, who was a sister of Theban Cadmus. She, the wicked step-mother, blinded Cleopatra's two sons.

(This might be a suitable place in which to offer a brief comment on the ode that refers to these three myths. At first sight it may seem both disjointed and frigid, especially as it occurs at so poignant a moment in the play. This judgement, however, may not be the correct one. Sophocles has his good dramatic reasons for keeping this sage, political chorus on Creon's side until Teiresias comes in to frighten them all; therefore he will not use his chorus at this moment for giving any direct expression to the feelings we all have, in the theatre, about Creon's monstrous treatment of Antigone: he gives them, instead, indirect expression. The ode is permeated by the ideas of darkness and cruelty. Of the three victims, the first was innocent, the second guilty. What about Antigone? As we ask – perhaps seeing Creon, who remains in full view during the ode – we hear of Eidothea's insensate cruelty and of the blind eyes 'that cried for vengeance'. Very soon Teiresias enters. Especially if we can allow something for the effect of the music and the dance, we may conclude that the ode is not exactly frigid.)

DIONYSUS receives an appeal from the chorus twice: a joyful one at the end of the first ode, a desperate one in the sixth. He figures here not particularly as god of the vine (still less as the god in whose honour the dramatic festival was being held), but pre-eminently as a god of Thebes. His mother, Semele, was one of Cadmus' daughters.

NIOBE, 'all tears', to whom Antigone compares herself, was born in Asia Minor, daughter of Tantalus, therefore sister of Pelops, and married Amphion of Thebes. She boasted that she had borne more children than Leto, whereupon Leto's children, who were Apollo and Artemis, killed all of Niobe's. She retired to her native Sipylus, was turned to stone, and weeps for ever.